PARLE

(Guide Pratique pour Touristes)

SPEAK CREOLE

(A Tourist Guide)

James Burty DAVID

Lilette DAVID

Clarel SEENYEN

EDITIONS DE L'OCEAN INDIEN

Published by
Editions de l'océan Indien
Stanley, Rose Hill
Mauritius
www.eoi-info.com

First published : 1988
Reprint: 1994, 1996
Revised edition : 1999
New revised edition : (2007)
Reprinted : (2010) by Toppan Security Printing Pte. Ltd.
Reprinted : Ajanta Offset & Packagings Ltd (2014)
Reprinted : Ajanta Offset & Packagings Ltd (2019)

ISBN 978-99903-0-571-5

Sommaire/Table of Contents

Comment utiliser le livre

- L'objectif de ce livre est de vous aider à vous initier au créole mauricien, à le comprendre et à l'utiliser dans des situations de communication.

- Le livre comporte une liste de thèmes/situations répondant à vos besoins pendant votre séjour chez nous, à Maurice.

- Pour chaque thème/situation on vous propose des phrases/éléments de phrase que vous pourrez utiliser pour exprimer vos besoins, pour parler aux Mauriciens, pour comprendre ce qu'ils vous disent et pour vous faire comprendre d'eux également.

- La table des matières vous indique le thème auquel vous avez à vous reporter pour trouver la/les phrase/s dont vous avez besoin. Tournez à la page qu'il vous faut.

- Les phrases de la colonne de gauche sont en français et en anglais; celles de la colonne de droite proposent l'équivalent en créole.

- On vous aide, dans la colonne de droite, à prononcer chaque phrase en créole par le biais des sons de votre langue.

- L'important ce n'est pas de prononcer le créole comme les gens du pays. L'essentiel c'est de comprendre et de se faire comprendre.

Pour découvrir l'île Maurice

- L'île Maurice se trouve dans l'Océan Indien. Elle se situe à un peu plus d'un millier de kilomètres de la côte est du continent africain. L'île couvre une superficie d'environ 1864 km^2.

- Port Louis est la capitale de l'île Maurice.

- L'île est indépendante depuis le 12 mars 1968, après avoir appartenu aux français d'abord et aux anglais après. Elle fait partie des pays du Commonwealth et de la Francophonie.

- L'Hôtel du Gouvernement, siège du pouvoir politique, se situe dans la capitale.

- L'aéroport de Plaisance se trouve au sud-est de l'île, dans le district de Grand Port près de Mahébourg.

- L'île comporte plus de 1,2 million d'habitants. C'est une société multiraciale où se côtoient des gens d'ethnies, de cultures et de langues différentes : les Nations Unies en miniature.

- L'unité monétaire légale est la roupie (Rs) qui est divisée en 100 sous.

Le Créole Mauricien

(ses particularités)

Cette rubrique donne une vue globale du créole mauricien. Elle n'est cependant pas d'une importance telle qu'elle nécessite d'être à tout prix mémorisée. Une simple lecture suffit.

- Le créole mauricien dérive du français mais il a évolué, au fil des années, pour devenir une langue à part entière.

- Il reste, à bien des égards, assez proche du français surtout en ce qui concerne le vocabulaire.

- Cependant, on trouve en créole, comme c'est le cas dans bien d'autres langues, des mots/termes empruntés à d'autres langues.

Exemples:

- **baksiss**, de l'arabe **bakchich**, qui veut dire **en prime.**
- **fuluss**, de l'arabe, qui veut dire **argent.**
- **jalsa,** mot indien, qui veut dire **fête.**
- **filling,** mot anglais, qui veut dire **station-service.**
- fer enn **booking**, **booking** mot anglais, qui veut dire **réservation.**

Tous ces termes font partie intégrante du créole mauricien et expliquent du même coup tout ce qui fait la richesse de cette langue.

- Un très grand nombre de mots créoles, malgré leur orthographe différente, se prononcent comme en français.

Créole	**Français**
dansé	danser
sauté	sauter

On retrouve aussi en créole des mots qui se prononcent différemment en français mais qui gardent toujours le même sens.

Exemples:

manzé	manger
zardin	jardin

D'autres mots français existent en créole mais avec un sens différent.

Exemples:

- **sapé** en créole veut dire **avoir de la chance**. Par contre le verbe **saper** en français a le sens de **ébranler** comme dans **saper la confiance de quelqu'un.**
- **medsinn** en créole avec le sens de **médicament** et ce n'est que quand il est accompagné de **la** comme dans **la medsinn** qu'il a le même sens qu'en français.
- **casse enn fler,** qui veut dire **cueillir une fleur.**

On retrouve aussi des archaïsmes. Alors que le sens des mots ci-dessous a évolué en France, il est resté figé à Maurice.

Exemples:

Créole	**Français**
gazet (gazette)	journal
sagrin (chagrin)	triste
plim (plume)	stylo

On assiste aussi en créole au phénomène du "suremploi"'. Le verbe **konné** (connaître) en créole se subsititue souvent au verbe **savoir** en français en sus de son emploi normal.

Exemples:

Créole	**Français**
Mo konne li	Je le connais
Mo konne dansé	Je sais danser.

Le phénomène est le même dans le cas du mot **pied,** employé en France dans un contexte restreint, comme dans un **pied de**

vigne. En créole **pyé**, par contre, veut dire **arbre** au lieu d'avoir uniquement le sens de **petit arbre.**

- Le verbe **largué** en créole, du français **larguer,** remplace quant à lui, le verbe **lâcher.** Terme marin au départ avec le sens de **lâcher les amarres,** il a évolué en créole pour avoir, indifféremment des contextes, le sens de l**âcher.**

- Dû à l'absence de certains sons, il existe des mots en créole qui peuvent avoir des sens différents en fonction de chaque contexte.

Exemples:

Créole	**Français**
pi	pis, pus
dé	deux, dé
ni	ni, nu
sou	sou, chou
sez	seize, chaise
mousse	mousse, mouche
ri	rue, riz
pli	pluie, pli, plus
caze	case, cage

- La grammaire du créole mauricien a, elle aussi, ses spécificités. Elle se démarque nettement de celle du français.

- En créole un même mot peut être tantôt un pronom, tantôt un adjectif.

Exemples:

Créole	**Français**
Mo	Je, mon
To	Tu, ton
Nu	Nous, nos
Ou	Vous (singulier), votre
Zot	Ils/Elles, leurs, vous (pluriel), vos

- Le pronom créole **li** est traduit tantôt par **il/elle** et tantôt par **lui.**

- Les verbes, quant à eux, ne se conjuguent pas aux différentes personnes mais la notion de **temps de verbe** existe.

- Autre fait important c'est le phénomène de l'amalgame de l'article et du nom.

Exemples:

Créole	**Français**
latab	table
dipin	pain
aine dipin	un pain
delo	eau
la porte	porte
lisyen	chien
mo lisyen	mon chien

- Ce phénomène ne concerne cependant pas tous les noms.

Exemples:

Créole	**Français**
- *ver*	verre
- *aine ver*	un verre
- *mosate*	mon chat
- *sez*	chaise
- *kayé*	cahier

Autant de particularités qui font du créole mauricien une langue en pleine expansion.

How to use the guide-book

- The aim of this guide-book is to help you to become acquainted with the Mauritian Creole, to understand it and use it for communication purposes.

- The booklet includes a variety of themes/situations that will meet your needs during your stay in our Island of Mauritius.

- In connection with each theme/situation there are several sentences/phrases that are provided to enable you express your needs and communicate with the Mauritians successfully and intelligibly.

- The Table of Contents indicates the appropriate theme of reference where you will find the desired utterance(s). Turn to the page indicated.

- The utterances on the left-hand side are in French and English; those on the right-hand side give the equivalent in Creole.

- In the right column you are also assisted with sounds of your own language. It will be easier for you to pronounce the sentences in Creole.

- What matters actually is not to pronounce Creole as the natives.

Discovering Mauritius

- Mauritius lies in the Indian Ocean. It is situated at about 1000 kilometres off the eastern coast of the African continent. The island occupies an area of about 1,864 square kilometres.

- Port Louis is the capital of Mauritius.

- The island has been independent since 12 March 1968. Before that, it had first belonged to the French, then to the British. It forms part of the Commonwealth and Francophone countries.

- Government House, which is the seat of political power, is to be found in the capital.

- Plaisance airport is situated in the south-east of the island, in the district of Grand Port, near Mahebourg.

- The island population has reached over 1.2 million inhabitants.

- It is a multi-racial society where people of different races, cultures and languages mix together: the United Nations in miniature.

- The legal currency is the rupee (Rs) which is divided into 100 cents.

The Mauritian Creole

(Its distinctive characteristics)

This section gives a general outline of the Mauritian Creole. It is, however, not so important to be actually memorized. It suffices to read it once.

- Mauritian Creole is derived from French but, over the years, it has undergone a certain evolution to finally become a language of its own.

- Notwithstanding, it remains in many respects quite close to French especially as concerns the vocabulary.

However, one can find in Creole, as in the case with many other languages, words/terms borrowed from other languages.

Examples:

- **baksiss,** from the Arabic word **bakchich**, which means **bonus.**
- **fuluss,** from the Arabic word, meaning **money.**
- **jalsa**, an Indian word, meaning **festivity.**
- **filling**, an English word meaning **filling station.**
- **fer enn booking, 'booking'** another English word for **reservation.**

All these terms form an integral part of the Mauritian Creole and thus give an idea of the copiousness of this tongue.

- Many a word in Creole, despite the difference in spelling, is pronounced as in French.

Exemples:

Créole	**Français**	**English**
dan-say	danser	to dance
soh-tay	sauter	to jump

- There also exist in Creole words derived from French but with a different pronunciation. Their meaning, however, is exactly the same as in French.

Examples:

Créole	**Français**	**English**
man-zay	manger	to eat
zar-dein	jardin	garden

- There are other French words which appear in Creole but with a different meaning.

Examples:

– **Sah-pay** in Créole means "**avoir de la chance**' **(to be lucky)**. In French, however, the verb **saper** has the sense of **ébranler (to sap)** as **in saper la confiance de quelqu'un (to sap someone's trust, i.e. to betray his trust).**

– **Medsinn** in Creole with the sense of **médicament (drug)**. It is only when it is preceded by **lah** as in **lah medsinn** that it assumes the same meaning as in French. In English it then refers to **medicine** as a science.

– **Kass enn flair, kass** which means **cueillir une fleur (to pluck a flower).**

- Another characteristic of Creole is archaism. Whereas the sense of the words below has evolved in France, it has remained static in Mauritius.

Examples:

Créole	**Français**	**English**
gah-zett (gazette)	journal	newspaper
sag-rein (chagrin)	triste	sad
plim (plume)	stylo	pen

◗ Creole is also featured by what might be called the phenomenon of 'over-exploitation'. The verb **koh-nay** in Creole, from the French verb **connaître (to know)**, is simply over-exploited in many contexts as a substitute for the French verb **savoir** in addition to its normal use, i.e. when it actually translates the verb **connaître.**

Examples:

Créole	**Français**	**English**
moh konn-lee	Je le/la connais	I know him/her
moh konn dan-say	Je sais danser	I know how to dance

◗ The same phenomenon applies to the word **pied** which is used in French but with a diminutive sense as in u**n pied de vigne** (**a small vine/the shoot of a vine)**. In Creole, however, **pee-yeah** simply means **arbre (tree)** instead of having the diminutive sense of **petit arbre (small tree/shoot).**

On the other hand, the verb **lar-gay** in Creole, from the French **larguer,** actually translates the French verb **lâcher (to untie/to let go)**. Originally a term pertaining to the sea with the sense of **lâcher les amarres (to untie the moorings),** this French verb **larguer,** on passing into Creole, has enlarged in meaning to assume indiscriminately the sense of **lâcher (to untie).**

◗ Owing to the non-existence of certain sounds, there are words in Creole that can have different meanings depending on the context.

Examples:

Créole	**Français**	**English**
pee	pis, pus	worse,pus
day	deux, dé	two, thimble
nee	ni, nu	neither,naked
soo	sou, chou	cent, cabbage
says	seize, chaise	sixteen, chair
mooss	mousse, mouche	moss, fly
ree	rue, riz	street, rice
plee	pluie, pli, plus	rain, fold, no more
caze	case, cage	hut, cage

◗ The grammar of the Mauritian Creole has also its own specific features. It stands in sharp contrast with the French one.

◗ In Creole, one same word can be now a pronoun, now an adjective.

Examples:

Créole	**Français**	**English**
moh	je, mon	I, my
toh	tu,ton	you, your
noo	nous, nos	we, our
hoo	vous (singulier) votre	you (singular) your
zot	ils/elles, leur(s)	they, their
	vous (pluriel), vos	your (plural), your

- The Creole pronoun **lee** is translated sometimes by **il/elle (he/she)** and sometimes by **lui (him/her).**

- As for the verbs, they are non conjugated in the different persons but the notion of **tenses** does exist.

- Another important feature is the peculiar merging of the article and the noun.

Examples:

Créole	**Français**	**English**
lah-tabb	table	table
dee-pein	pain	bread
aine dee-pein	un pain	a loaf
dee-loh	eau	water
lah-port	porte	door
lee-see-hein	chien	dog

This phenomenon does not, however, apply to all the nouns.

Examples:

Créole	**Français**	**English**
vair	verre	glass
aine vair	un verre	a glass
moh sat	mon chat	my cat
says	chaise	chair
kah-yeah	cahier	exercise-book

These many characteristics do make of the Mauritian Creole a fully dynamic language.

Quelques expressions de la vie de tous les jours/ Some expressions of every day life

Bonjour, ça va? *Good morning, how are you?*	Bonjour, ça va? *Bon-zoor, sah vah?*
Salut! *Hello/Hi!*	Salut! *Ah-low!*
Que faites vous aujourd'hui? *What do you do today?*	Qui ou faire zordi? *Kee hoo fair zor-dee?*
Vous avez eu du courrier? *Do you have any letters?*	Ou fine gagne laite? *Hoo feen gah-ee let?*
Vous avez chaud? *Do you feel hot?*	Ou gagne soh? *Hoo gah-ee soh?*
A partir de maintenant. *As from now.*	Astère la *Ass-tair lah.*
A tout à l'heure. *See you later.*	Talère. *Tah-lair.*
De mon temps. *In my time.*	Dans mo lé temps. *Dan moh lay tan.*
Combien de temps faut-il pour.. *How long will it take to... ?*	Comié lé temps pou prend pou...? *Koh-mee-yeah lay tan poo pran poo...?*
Vous avez l'heure? *Do you have the time?*	Ou éna lère? *Hoo hay-nah lair?*
Vous vous amusez bien? *You're enjoying yourself well?*	Ou pé amize ou bien? *Hoo pay ha-meez hoo bee-yen?*
C'est formidable/super. *That's great.*	Formidabe. *For-mee-dab.*
De rien/Je vous en prie. *Don't mention it.*	Pas de quoi. *Pad-kwah.*
Ça ne fait rien. *It doesn't matter.*	Pas faire nan-nien. *Pah fair nan-nyen.*

Je suis à vous dans un instant.
I'll be at your service in a moment.

Mo guette ou aine ti mama.
Moh gait hoo an tee mah-mah

Désolé. Je suis en retard.
Sorry. I'm late.

Sorie, mo en rétar.
Sorry, moh en ray-tar.

A plus tard.
See you later.

Mo trouve toi talère.
Mon troov twah tah-lair.

Quel est le coût de la vie ici?
What's the cost of living here?

Qui coût de la vie ici?
Kee kood la-vee hee-see?

Parlez plus haut.
Speak up.

Cause pli fort.
Koze plee for.

C'est une façon de parler.
It is a way of speaking.

C'est aine façon causé
Say hen fahsson kozay.

Qu'est-ce que vous en dîtes?
What do you say to that?

Qui ou dire?
Kee hoo deer?

N'en parlons plus.
Let us say no more about it

Laisse nou pas cause sa.
Layss noo pah koze sah.

Comme on dit...
As it is said that...

Coma dire...
Koh-mah deer...

On dit que...
It is said ...

Zotte dire qui...
Zott deer kee...

Que dites-vous?
What do you say?

Qui ou dire?
Kee hoo deer?

Ça vous ennuie?
Does that annoy you ?

Ça pé agace ou?
Sah pay ha-gas hoo?

Ça vous plaît?
Does it please you?

Sa plaire ou?
Sah plair hoo?

Les gens disent que...
People say that...

Dimoune dire qui...
Dee-moon deer kee...

A mon avis...
In my opinion

Selon moi
Say-lon mwa

Changer d'avis
To change opinion

Sanze l'opinion
Sanz low-pee-neeon

A quoi pensez-vous?
What are you thinking of?

Qui ou pé pensé?
Kee hoo pay pan-say?

Eh bien!
Well!

Abé
Ah-bay

C'est à votre goût?
Do you like it?

Ou content li?
Hoo-kon-tan lee?

Soyez sans crainte.
Have no fear.

Pas bizin père.
Pah bee-zein pair.

Ne vous tourmentez pas.
Don't worry.

Pas bizin tracassé.
Pah bee-zein trah-kass-say.

Ne vous mettez pas en colère.
Don't be angry.

Pas bizin faire colère.
Pah bee-zein fair koh-lair.

Faites de votre mieux.
Do your best.

Faire ou mié possib.
Fair hoo mee-yeah poh-sib.

On vous demande.
You are wanted.

Pé rode ou.
Pay rod hoo.

Je n'ose pas
I dare not

Mo pas osé.
Moh pah ho-zay.

Quelle audace!
How dare you!

Qui l'audace!
Kee loh-dass.

Je n'y peux rien.
I can't help it.

Mo pas capave faire nan-nien.
Moh pah kah-pav fair nan-nyen.

Insulter quelqu'un
To call someone names.

Insilté kikaine.
Hein-sil-tay kick-hen.

Je regrette...
I'm sorry...

Mo regretté
Moh ray-grait-hey.

Enchanté?
How do you do?

Qui manière?
Kee mah-nee-yeeair?

Heureux de vous avoir rencontré
Pleased to have met you.

Mo content mo fine zoine ou
Moh contan moh feen zo-hen hoo.

Je suis heureux d'être venu.
It pleases me to have come.

Mo content mo fine vini.
Moh contan moh feen vee-nee

A la prochaine! *See you soon.*	La prossaine fois. *Lah pro-senne fwa.*
On peut entrer s'il vous plaît? *May I come in, please?*	Capave rentré s'il vous plaît? *Kah-pav ran-tray seel-voo-play?*
Est-il permis de se garer ici? *Is it allowed to park here?*	Capave park loto ici? *Kah-pav park loh-toh hee-see?*
Est-ce qu'on peut pêcher dans ce coin? *Can we fish in this place?*	Capave la pesse ici? *Kah-pav lah pess he-see?*
Je peux emprunter ce chemin? *Can I take this path ?*	Capave passe par la ? *Kah-pav pahss par lah?*
Je peux vous emprunter ceci? *May l borrow this from you?*	Capave prend sa prêté are ou? *Kah-pav pran sah pray-tay are hoo?*
Par où doit-on sortir? *Where is the exit?*	Cotte capave sorti? *Kot ka-pav sor-tee?*
Où peut-on téléphoner? *Where is there a telephone ?*	Cotte capave téléphoné? *Kot ka-pav tay-lay-phonay?*
Je peux laisser mes affaires ici? *May I leave my things here?*	Mo capave laisse mo banne zaffaires ici? *Mo ka-pav less moh ban zah-fair he-see?*
Le bus passe normalement toutes les heures. *Normally, there is a bus every hour.*	Bisse passe normalement sak ine hère tan. *Bis pahss normal-man sak in hair tan*
Frappez *Knock*	Tapé *Tah-pay*
Défense de fumer. *No smoking.*	Pas fimé. *Pah fee-may.*
Interdiction de se garer. *No parking.*	Pas park ici. *Pah park hee-see.*
Réservé aux taxis *Taxis only.*	Parking zisse pou taxi ici *Parking ziss poo taxi hee-see.*
Parking. *Car park.*	Parking *Parking*

Se présenter et converser avec quelqu'un/Introducing oneself to somebody and conversing with him

Comment s'y prendre/How to go about it

Salut/Bonjour *Hello/Good morning*	Bonzour *Bon-zoor*
Je suis Monsieur/Madame X *My name is Mr/Mrs X*	Mo appelle Missié/Madame *Moh ha-pel Mee-see-yeah/Madam*
J'apprends le créole. *I'm learning creole.*	Mo pé apranne créole *Moh pay ap-rand cray-ol*
Je suis Française, je viens de la Région de ... *I am French, I come from the Region of ...*	Mo aine française, mo sorti ... *Moh enn Fran-says, moh sor-tee ...*
Comment vous appelez-vous? *What is your name?*	Coma ou appélé? *Ko-mah hoo ha-pay-lay?*
Vous venez de quelle ville/quel village? *Which town/village do you come from?*	Qui la ville/Qui villaz ou sorti? *Kee lah-vil/kee vee-laz hoo sor-tee?*
Vous êtes de l'Angleterre? *Are you from England?*	Ou sorti l'Angleterre? *Hoo sor-tee lang-lay-tair?*
Je suis un touriste. *I am a tourist*	Mo aine touriste *Moh an tourist*
Vous êtes marié/ée? *Are you married?*	Ou marié? *Hoo mar-yeah?*
Je suis célibataire/marié. *I am single/I am married.*	Mo aine célibataire/mo marié. *Moh an say-lee-bah-tair/moh mar-yeah.*

French / English	Creole / Pronunciation
Voici ... *This is...*	Ala ... *Halah...*
mon mari *my husband*	mo mari *moh mah-ree*
ma femme *my wife*	mo femme/mo madame *moh famm/moh madam*
ma fille *my daughter*	mo tifi *moh tee-fee*
mon fils *my son*	mo garçon *moh gar-son*
mon ami/amie *my friend*	mo camarade *moh kah-mah-rad*
Avez-vous des enfants? *Do you have any children?*	Ou éna zenfants? *Hoo hay-nah zan-fan?*
Je n'ai pas d'enfant. *I haven't any children.*	Mo péna zenfants *Moh pay-nah zan-fan*
J'habite Londres. *I live in London.*	Mo reste Londes. *Mo rayste Londe.*
J'habite ... *I live*	Mo reste ... *Moh rayste ...*
à Rose-Hill *at Rose-Hill*	Rose-Hill *Rose-Hill*
à Quatre-Bornes *at Quatre-Bornes*	Katte-Borne *Cat-Born*
à Port-Louis *in Port-Louis*	Port-Louis *Port-Louis*
dans le nord de l'île *in the north of the island*	dans lé nord *dan lay nor*
Comment allez-vous?/ça va? *How do you do?*	Comment ça va? *Ko-man sah-vah?*
Enchanté de vous rencontrer. *Please to meet you.*	Mo content monne zoine ou. *Moh kon-tan monn zwen hoo.*

French / English	Creole / Pronunciation
Je suis ici ... *I am here ...*	Mo ici ... *Moh hee-see ...*
en vacances *on holiday*	pou vacance *poo vah-kanss*
pour affaires *on business*	pou bise-nesse *poo business*
Vous restez longtemps ici? *Are you staying long here?*	Ou pou reste longtemps ici? *Hoo poo rayste lon-tan hee-see?*
C'est la première fois que vous venez à Maurice? *Is it your first visit to Mauritius?*	Prémié fois ou vine Maurice? *Pray-mee-yeah fwa hoo veen Moh-reess?*
Puis-je parler à ...? *May I speak to ...?*	Mo capave cause avec/ek ...? *Moh kah-pav koze hah-vek?*
Comment voyez-vous Maurice? *How do you like Mauritius?*	Comment ou trouve Maurice? *Ko-mah hoo troov Moh-reess?*
Comment sont les gens? *How do you find the people?*	Comment dimoune été? *Ko-man dee-moon hay-tay?*
Il y a combien d'habitants dans l'île? *What is the population of the island?*	Comié dimoune éna dans l'île? *Ko-mee-yeah dee-moon hay-nah dan leel?*
Il fait chaud à cette période de l'année? *Is it hot at this time of the year?*	Faire so sa période lannée-là. *Fair soh sah period lahnay-lah.*
Quel temps fait-il chez vous? *What's the weather like in your country?*	Qui lé temps faire cotte ou? *Kee lay tan fair kot hoo?*
Vous parlez combien de langues? *How many languages do you speak?*	Ou cause comié langaze? *Hoo koze ko-mee-yeah lan gaz?*

Quelle est la langue officielle du pays?
What's the official language of the country?

Qui la langue officiel pays?
Kee lah lang hoh-fee-see-el pay-hee?

Je vais bien.
I am fine.

Mo bien
Moh bee-yen

Je compte y rester deux semaines/ quinze jours/deux ou trois semaines.
I intend to stay her for two weeks/ a fortnight/a couple of weeks.

Mo éna l'intention reste pou reste dé sémaines/quinze zours/ dé trois semaines.
Moh hay-nah lein-tan-see-on rayste poo rayste day saymen/ kinze zoor/day trwa say-men.

C'est ma première visite chez vous.
It's my first visit to your country.

Mo premié visite ici.
Moh pray-mee-yeah visit hee-see.

Je trouve votre île belle.
I find your island beautiful.

Mo trouve ou pays zoli.
Moh troov hoo pay-hee zoh-lee.

Les gens sont sympa/gentils.
The people are nice/friendly.

Banne dimounes zentils.
Bann dee-moon zan-tee.

Il y a plus d'un million de Mauriciens.
There are over one million Mauritians.

Ena plisse ki aine million Mauriciens.
Hay-nah ha pleess ki hen mee-lee-on Moh-ree-see-en.

Il ne fait pas trop chaud ces jours-ci.
It's not very hot at present.

Pas faire trop so astère-là.
Pah fair troh soh ass-tair-lah.

Les Mauriciens parlent plusieurs langues.
Mauritians speak several languages.

Banne Mauriciens cause boucoup langaze.
Bann moh-ree-see-en koze boo-koo lan-gaz.

La langue officielle c'est l'anglais.
The official language is English.

La langue officiel anglais.
Lah lang ho-fee-see-el ang-lay.

Demander son chemin/Asking one's way

Quoi dire/What to say

S'il vous plaît! (pour attirer l'attention du passant). *Excuse me! (to draw the passer's by attention).*	S'il vous plaît! *Ex-kize mwa!*
Pour aller ...? *How do I get ...?*	Pou alle...? *Poo hal ...?*
à la plage *to the beach*	la plage *lah plaz*
à la mairie *to the townhall*	minisipalité *mee-nee-see-pa-lee-tay*
au bureau de change *to the change bureau*	biro sanze casse *bee-ro sanz cass*
au stade *to the sports stadium*	stade *stad*
au centre ville *to the town centre*	en ville *sant lah vil*
à la rue Royale *to Royal Road*	la ri Royal *lah ree Rwa-yal*
à Marie Reine de la Paix *to Marie Reine de la Paix*	Marie Reine dé la Pé *Marie Renn day lah Pay*
aux Champ de Mars *to Champ de Mars*	Sanne marse *Sann Mars*
Où se trouve ...? *Where is ...?*	Cotte ...? *Kot ...?*
C'est loin ...? *Is it far from here?*	Li loin ...? *Lee lwen ...?*
la gare d'autobus *the bus station*	la gare bisse *lah gar biss*
le musée *the museum*	mizé *mee-zay*
Il y a encore loin à aller? *Is there still a long way to go?*	Ena encor loin pou allé? *Hay-nah han-kor lwen poo allay?*

On est prêt d'arriver? *Are we about to be there?*	Nou pré pou arrivé? *Noo pray poo arrivay?*
On peut y aller à pied? *Can we walk up there?*	Nou capave alle marsé? *Noo kah-pav hal mar-say?*
Vous pouvez répéter s'il vous plaît? *Could you please repeat it?*	Ou capave rédire s'il vous plaît? *Hoo kah-pav ray-deer seel-voo-play?*
Je ne comprends pas. *I don't understand.*	Mo pas comprend. *Moh pah kon-pran.*
Je n'ai rien compris. *I haven't understood anything at all.*	Mo pas fine comprend nan-rien. *Moh pah finn kon-pran nan-nyen.*
Je n'ai rien entendu. *I haven't heard anything at all.*	Mo pas fine tanne nan-nien. *Moh pah finn tann nan-nyen.*
Ça y est. J'ai compris. *It's OK! I've got it now.*	Oké. Mo fine comprend. *OK. Moh finn kon-pran.*
Est-ce qu'il y a près d'ici …? *Is there … nearby?*	Eski ena près par ici …? *Ess-kee ena pray par ee-see …?*
une quincaillerie *a hardware shop*	aine quincaillerie *hen ken-ka-yee-ree*
un pressing *a dry cleaner*	Draille kli-ning *Dry cleaning*
un arrêt d'autobus *a bus stop*	biss stop *biss stop*
des WC publics *a public toilet*	toilettes piblik *twa-let pee-blick*
une pâtisserie *a cake shop*	aine pâtisserie *enn pah-tiss-ree*
un marchand de journaux *a newsagent's*	aine marsan la gazette *enn marsan lah-ga-zet*
J'ai perdu mon chemin *I've lost my way.*	Mo fine perdi mo simain *Moh finn per-dee moh see-mein.*

Réponses probables/Likely answers

Continuez tout droit ... *Go on straight*	Continié droite *Kon-tee-nee-yeah-ah drawt*
Prenez la deuxième à gauche *Take the second street on your left*	Contourne ségon la ri à gosse *Kon-toorne say-gon lah ree ah goss*
Allez jusqu'au carrefour ... *Go as far as the cross-roads*	Alle ziska la croisé simain. *Hal zee-skah lah krwa-zay see-men*
Continuez jusqu'au rond-point ... *Push on up/down to the round-about ...*	Alle ziska rond-point ... *Hal zee-skah ron-pwen ...*
Vous tournez à droite ... *Turn right ...*	Tourne à droite ... *Toorne ah drwat ...*
Continuez jusqu'aux feux, puis vous prenez la première à gauche... *Go up to the traffic-light, then you take the first on the left ...*	Alle ziska robot, après tourne premier la ri à gosse ... *Hal zee-ska robo, ah-pray toorne pray-mee-yeeah lah ree ah goss ...*

A L'HÔTEL / AT THE HOTEL

Quoi dire/what to say

Puis-je faire une réservation? *Can I make a reservation?*	Mo capave faire aine réservation? *Moh kah-pav fair an ray-zer-vah-see-hon?*
Puis-je réserver une chambre pour deux personnes? *Can I book a room for two persons?*	Mo capave réserve aine la samme pou dé dimoune? *Moh kah-pav ray-zerve hen lah-samm pou day dee-moon?*
Avez-vous des chambres libres? *Have you any vacancies?*	Ou éna la samme libe? *Hoo hay-nah lah samm leeb?*
A quel hôtel vas-tu descendre? *At which hotel are you putting up?*	Qui l'hotel ou pou allé? *Kee loh-tell hoo poo allay?*
J'ai une réservation. *I have a booking.*	Mo éna aine réservation. *Moh hay-nah an ray-zer-vah-see-hon.*
Je n'ai pas de réservation. *I don't have a reservation.*	Mo péna réservation. *Moh pay-nah ray-zer-vah-see-hon.*
Où trouver à se loger? *Where to find accommodation?*	Cotte pou alle resté? *Kot poo hal rayss-tay?*
Je voudrais … *I would like to have …*	Mo oulé *Moh hoo-lay …*
une chambre *a room*	aine la samme *an lah samm*
deux chambres *two rooms*	dé la samme *day lah samm*
une chambre avec tout le confort *a room with every comfort*	aine la samme avec tout confort *an lah samm ah-vek too confor*

French	Creole
un appartement *a suite*	aine l'appartement *an lah-part-man*
une chambre à deux lits *a double-bedded room*	aine la samme avec dé lili *an lah samme ah-vek day lee-lee.*
une chambre avec un berceau *a room with a cot*	aine la samme avec aine bère *an lah samme ah-vek an bair*
une chambre avec WC *a room with a toilet*	aine la samme avec toilette *an lah samme ah-vek twah-let*
une chambre avec douche *a room with a shower*	aine la samme avec dousse *an la samm ah-vek dooss*
une chambre avec la salle de bains *a room with a bathroom*	aine la samme avec salle dé bain *an la samm ah-vek sall day ben*
une chambre avec balcon *a room with a balcony*	aine la samme avec balcon *an lah samm ah-vek bal-kon*
une chambre pour trois semaines *a room for three weeks*	aine la samme pour trois sémaines *an lah samm poo trwah say-mein*
une chambre pour une nuit *a room for one night*	aine la samme pou aine la nuite *an lah samm poo an lah nweet*

French	Creole
Je voulais … *I would like …*	Mo oulé *Moh hoo-lay …*
une pension de famille *a boarding house*	aine pension fami *an pan-see-on fah-mee*
une pension complète *a full board*	aine pension complet *an pan-see-on kom-play*
une chambre et petit déjeuner *bed and breakfast*	aine la samme ek ti dézéné *an lah samm eck tee day-zay-nay*

Je préfère une chambre sur le devant/à l'arrière *I'd prefer a room at the front/at the back.*	Mo préfère aine la samme par dévan/par derrière. *Moh pray-fair an lah samm par day-van/par day-ree-hair.*
Je préfère une chambre donnant sur la rue. *I prefer a room facing the street.*	Mo préfère aine la samme qui tomme lor la rie. *Moh pray-fair an lah samm kee tom lor lah ree.*
Je peux voir la chambre? *Can I look at the room?*	Mo capave guette la samme la? *Moh kap-have gait lah samme lah?*
Ça me plaît. Je la prends. *I like this one. I'll take it.*	Mo d'accord. Mo prend li. *Moh dak-or. Moh pran lee.*
Ça ne me convient pas. *This doesn't suit me.*	Mo pas d'accord are li. *Moh pah dak-or are lee.*
Vous pouvez faire monter mes bagages/descendre mes bagages? *Could you take up/take down my luggage.*	Ou capave faire monte mo ba-gaz/désanne mo ba-gaz? *Hoo kah-pav faire mont moh bag-haz/day-sann moh bag-haz?*
Puis-je voir …? *May I see …?*	Mo capave guette …? *Moh kah-pav gait …?*
l'hôtelier *the hotel-keeper*	responsable l'hotel *rayss-pon-sab loh-tell*
le gérant *the manager*	zérant *manager*
la gérante *the manageress*	zérante *manager*
Dois-je remplir le bulletin d'arrivée? *Do I have to fill in the arrival form?*	Mo bizin rempli aine forme d'arrivée? *Moh bees-hein ram-plee an form dah-ree-vay.*
Quel est le prix global? *What is the inclusive price?*	Qui prix global? *Kee pree gloh-bal?*

French / English	Creole / Pronunciation
Vous faites aussi restaurant? *Do you serve meals as well?*	Ou servi manzé aussi? *Hoo sair-vee man-zay hoo-see?*
A quelle heure ...? *At what time ...?*	Qui lère ...? *Kee lair ...?*
passe la femme de chambre *comes the chambermaid?*	famme dé samme passé? *famm day samm pah-say?*
est le petit déjeuner *is breakfast*	ti dézéné *tee day-zay-nay*
est le dîner *is dinner*	dîner *dee-nay*
Je voudrais prolonger mon séjour ici. *I would like to stay longer here.*	Mo envie reste encore hein-pé. *Moh han-vee rayss han-kor hein-pay.*
Où est l'ascenseur? *Where is the lift?*	Kotte l'ascenseur? *Kot lah-sen-sair?*
Quel est le numéro de ma chambre? *What is my room number?*	Qui niméro mo la samme? *Kee nee-may-roh moh la samm?*
Je prendrai le petit déjeuner dans la chambre. *I'll have breakfast in my room.*	Mo pou prend mo ti dézné dans la samme. *Moh pou pran moh tee day-zay-nay dan lah sam.*
Avez-vous des cartes postales? *Do you have postcards?*	Ou éna cartes postales? *Hoo hay-nah cart postal?*
Y-a-t-il des messages pour moi? *Is there any message for me?*	Ena messazes pou moi? *Hay-nah may-sahze poo mwah?*
Puis-je avoir ...? *Can I have ...?*	Mo capave gagne ...? *Moh kah-pav gah-gne...?*
quelques cintres supplémentaires *a few more coat-hangers?*	dé trois porte manteaux han plisse *day-trwa port man-toh han pleess*
encore une couverture *another blanket*	encore aine molton *han-kor hen mol-ton*
deux autres verres *two more glasses*	dé lotte verres *day lot vair*

Apportez-moi de l'eau chaude, s'il vous plaît. *Bring me up some hot water, please?*	Ammène dilo so s'il vous plaît. *Ha-men dee-loh soh seel-voo-play?*
Pouvez-vous …? *Can you …?*	Ou capave …? *Hoo kah-pav …?*
vous occuper de mes vêtements *look after my clothes*	okipe mo linze *okip moh linze*
m'appeler un taxi *get me a taxi*	appelle aine taxi pou moi *hap-hell an taxi pou mwa*
me réveiller à 7 heures *wake me up at 7 o'clock*	lève moi sette haire *laiv mwa set hair*
me trouver un interprète *find me an interpreter*	rode aine interprète pou moi *rod an hein-tair-prait poo mwa*
La clé du trois, s'il vous plaît. *The key to number three, please.*	La clé la samme niméro trois s'il vous plaît *Lah clay lah samm nee-may-roh trwa seel-voo-play.*
Puis-je avoir un reçu …? *May I have a receipt?*	Mo capave gagne aine réssi. *Moh kah-pav gah-gne hen ray-see?*
L'hôtel est … *The hotel …*	L'hotel … *Loh-tel …*
bien tenu *is well kept*	bien propre *bee-yee-hein prop*
convenable *is convenient*	correk *correk*
bien fréquenté *receives a lot of customers*	éna boucoup clients *hay-nah boo-coo clee-yee-an*

Réactions probables/Likely reactions

Je regrette, tout est pris/occupé. *I'm sorry, there are no vacancies.*	Sorrie, partout okipé. *Sorry, par-too okee-pay.*
Je regrette, c'est complet. *Sorry, we're full.*	Sorry, foule partout. *Sorry, full par-too.*
Je n'ai qu'une chambre de libre. *There's only one room available.*	Mo éna aine sèle la samme libe. *Moh hay-nah hen sail lah samm leeb.*
Je n'ai rien d'autre. *That's all I have.*	Mo pas éna lotte. *Moh pah hay-nah lot.*
Avez-vous votre carte d'identité? *Have you your identity card?*	Ou éna ou carte d'identité? *Hoo hay-nah hoo cart dee-den-tee-tay?*
Vous voulez voir la chambre? *Do you want to have a look at the room?*	Ou lé guette la samme là? *Hoo lay gait lah samm lah?*
Pour combien de personnes? *For how many people?*	Pou comié dimoune? *Poo ko-mee-yeah dee-moon?*
Adressez-vous … *Apply at …*	Adresse ou … *Ha-drayss hoo …*
au bureau *the office*	biro *bee-roh*
à la direction *the management*	direction *dee-rek-see-hon*
Faites votre choix *Make your choice.*	Faire ou soit *Fair hoo swah.*
Il vous faut libérer la chambre avant midi. *You will have to vacate the room before noon.*	Ou bizin quitte la samme avant midi. *Hoo bees-hein kit lah samm ah-van mee-dee.*
Laissez vos bagages ici. *Leave your luggage here.*	Laisse ou bagaze ici. *Less hoo bah-gaz hee-see.*

A LA BANQUE/AT THE BANK

A quel comptoir aller, s'il vous plaît? vous plaît?
Which desk should I go to please?

Qui comptoir bizin allé s'il vous plaît?
Kee kon-twar bee-zen allay seel-voo-play?

Je voudrais changer … en roupies
I'd like to change … in rupees

Mo oulé sanze … en roupies.
Moh hoo-lay sanz … en roo-pee

ces euros
these euros

sa banne euros la
sah bann euros lah

ces francs suisses
these Swiss Francs

sa banne francs suisse la
sah bann fran Swiss lah

ces dollars
these dollars

sa banne dollars la
sah bann dollar lah

ces livres sterling
these pounds sterling

sa banne livre sterlain la
sah bann leeve sterling lah

Quel est le cours du change/ le taux de change?
What's the rate of exchange?

Qui valère sa casse là?
Kee vah-lair sah cass lah?

Je voudrais …
I'd like to …

Mo oulé …
Moh hoo-lay …

encaisser ce chèque
cash this cheque

sanze sa chèque la
sanz sah check lah

encaisser ces chèques de voyage
cash these travellers' cheques

sanze sa banne chèque voyaze la
sanz sah bann check voyaz lah.

Pouvez-vous me donner des coupures de cinquante roupies s'il vous plaît?
Could you please give me fifty rupee notes?

Ou capave donne moi coupire cinquante roupies, s'il vous plaît?
Hoo kah-pav donn mwa koo-peer cin-kant roo-pee seel-voo-play?

Tenez, voici mon passeport.
Look, here's my passport.

Ala mo passport.
Ah-lah moh passport.

Je voudrais ouvrir ... *I'd like to open ...*	Mo oulé ouvert ... *Moh hoo-lay hoo-vair ...*
un compte d'épargne *a savings account*	aine compte d'épargne *hen kont day-pargn*
un compte courant *a current account*	aine compte courant *hen kont koo-ran*
Quel est le taux d'intérêt? *What is the rate of interest?*	Qui so l'intérêt? *Kee soh lin-tay-ray?*
Pouvez-vous débiter mon compte de ... *Could you debit my account by ...*	Ou capave débite mon compte par ... *Hoo cah-pav day-bit moh kont par ...*
Je passe à la caisse? *I call at the pay-desk?*	Mo passe la caisse? *Moh pass lah kayss?*
C'est pour ... *It's for ...*	Pou ... *Poo ...*
un virement *a transfer*	aine virement *an trans-fair*
un prêt *a loan*	aine prêt *an loan*
un carnet de chèques *a cheque-book*	aine carnet chèque *an car-nay check*
un compte de dépôts *a deposit account*	aine compte dépots *an kont day-po*
un retrait *a withdrawal*	pou tire casse *poo teer kass*
arrêter un compte *closing an account*	pou ferme aine compte *poo fairm hen kont*
me porter caution pour ... *standing security for ...*	diboute caution pou ... *dee-boot ko-see-on poo ...*
Je signe où? *Where should I sign?*	Cotte mo signé? *Kot moh see-gnay?*
Quelles sont les heures d'ouverture, s'il vous plaît? *What are the opening hours please?*	Qui lère ouvert s'il vous plaît? *Kee lair hoo-vair seel-voo-play?*

French / English	Creole / Pronunciation
Où se trouve le distributeur automatique? *Where is the ATM machine?*	Kotte distribitère automatique la été? *Kot diss-tree-bee-tair automatic lah hay-tay?*
J'ai une carte de crédit. *I have a credit card.*	Mo éna aine carte crédit. *Moh hay-nah an cart cray-dee.*

Au restaurant/At the restaurant

French / English	Creole / Pronunciation
Je voudrais réserver une table … *I'd like to reserve a table …*	Mo lé réserve aine la tabe … *Moh lay ray-zairv hen lah tab*
pour quatre personnes *for four persons*	pou quate dimounes *poo cat dee-moon*
pour ce soir *for this evening*	pou à soir *poo ha swar*
J'ai déjà réservé. *I've already made a reservation.*	Mo fine fini réservé. *Moh finn fee-nee ray-zair-vay.*
Garçon! *Waiter!*	Garçon! *Garss-hon*
La carte, s'il vous plaît. *The menu, please.*	Méni, s'il vous plaît. *May-nee seel-voo-play.*
Le menu du jour. *Today's special menu.*	Méni di zour. *May-nee dee zoor.*
Le menu à prix fixe. *The fixed-price menu.*	Méni prix fixé. *May-nee pree fix-ay.*
Une tournée de boisson. *A round*	Aine tournée boire. *Hen toor-nay bwar.*
Payer une tournée. *To stand a round.*	Paye aine tournée. *Pay-ee hen toor-nay.*
Un dîner à trois services. *A three-course dinner.*	Aine dîné trois services. *Hen dee-nay trwa sair-veess.*
Le premier plat *The first course.*	Prémié plat. *Pray-mee-yeah plah.*

La carte des vins *The wine list.*	Carte divin *Cart dee-vein.*
Une carafe de vin. *A carafe of wine.*	Aine carafe divin. *Hen kah-raf dee-vein.*
Une demi-carafe de vin. *A half carafe of wine.*	Aine démi carafe divin. *Hen day-mee kah-raf dee-vein.*
Encore du vin. *Some more wine.*	Encore impé divin. *Han-kor imp-pay dee-vein.*
Qu'est-ce que c'est ça? *What's this?*	Qui si sa sa? *Kee see sah sah?*
Je voudrais essayer cela. *I would like to try this one.*	Mo envie seille sanne-la-la... *Moh han-vee say-he sann-lah-lah.*
Je voudrais commander … *I'd like to order …*	Mo lé commande … *Moh lay commann …*
des crevettes *shrimps*	crévettes *cray-vet*
des huîtres *oysters*	zuittes *zweet*
des langoustes *spring lobsters*	langousses *lang-ouss*
Je suis végétarien *I'm veg.*	Mo vézétarien. *Moh vay-zay-tah-rien*
Qu'avez-vous comme hors d'oeuvre? *What have you got as side-dishes?*	Qui ou éna comme hors dève? *Kee hoo hay-nah kom or-daiv?*
Je prendrai une salade ... *I'll have a salad ...*	Mo pou prend aine salade ... *Moh poo pran an salad*
de laitue *of lettuce*	léti *lay-tee*
de maïs *of maize*	maille *mah-yee*
de chou *of cabbage*	li sou *lee soo*
de concombre *of cucumber*	cocomme *kokomm*

French / English	Mauritian Creole / Pronunciation
J'ai envie d'une spécialité locale. *I would like to have a local dish.*	Mo envie aine manzé mauricien. *Moh han-vee an man-zay moh-ree-syain*
La cuisine mauricienne/chinoise/indienne *The Mauritian/Chinese/Indian cuisine*	La cousine mauricien/sinois/indien *Lah koo-zeen moh-ree-see-hein/see-nwa/hein-dee-hein*
du riz et du cari *rice and curry*	di riz ek cari *dee ree eck kah-ree*
un cari de poisson *a fish curry*	aine cari poisson *enn kah-ree pwah-sson*
poulet … *a chicken …*	poulet … *poo-lay …*
boeuf … *a beef …*	bèfe *baiff …*
mouton … *a mutton …*	mouton … *moo-ton …*
cabri … *a goat-meat*	cabri … *kah-bree …*
cerf … *a deer-meat …*	cerf … *serf …*
une daube de poisson *a fish daube*	aine la dobe poisson *an lah dob pwah-sson*
une daube de viande *a meat stew*	aine lah dobe la vianne *an lah dob lah viahnn*
une rougaille de viande *meat in tomato sauce*	aine rougaille la vianne *an roog-ha-yee lah viahnn*
une rougaille de poisson salé *salt-fish in tomato sauce*	aine rougaille poisson salé *an roog-ha-yee pwah-sson sah-lay*
une rougaille de crevettes *shrimps in tomato sauce*	aine rougaille crévette *an roog-ha-yee cray-vait*
un briani au poulet *a chicken biryani*	briani poulet *bree-ha-nee poo-lay*
un briani poisson *a fish biryani*	briani poisson *bree-ha-nee pwah-sson*

French	Creole
un briani cerf *a deer-meat biryani*	briani cerf *bree-ha-nee serf*
un briani aux légumes *a vegetable biryani*	briani léguime *bree-ha-nee leg-heem*
un bouillon de poisson *a fish broth*	bouillon poisson *boo-yon pwah-sson*
un bouillon de crabes *a crab broth*	bouillon crabe *boo-yon crabb*
un potage *a vegetable soup*	aine potaze *an poh-taz*
un chatini de pomme d'amour *a tomato chutney*	aine satini pomme d'amour *an sah-tee-nee pomm dah-moor*
un chatini coco *a coconut chutney*	aine satini coco *an sah-tee-nee coco*
un chatini cotomili *a coriander chutney*	aine satini cotomili *an sah-tee-nee co-toh-mee-lee*
un vindaye de poisson *a fish 'vindaye'*	aine vindaye poisson *an veen-dah-yee pwah-sson*
du poisson frit *fried fish*	poisson frire *pwahs-son freer*
un steak à point/saignant *un medium/underdone steak*	aine steck bien frire/saig-nant *an steak bee-hein freer/say-gnan*
un steak bien cuit *a well-done steak*	aine steck bien cuit *an steak bee-hein kwee*

French	Creole
C'est trop ... *It's too ...*	Li trop ... *Lee tro ...*
salé *salty*	salé *sah-lay*
épicé *spicy*	épicé *hay-pee-say*
sucré *sweet*	doux *doo*
aigre *sour*	aigue *egg*

brèdes à l'étouffée *stewed green*	brède touffée *brayd too-fay*
un sauté de petits pois *peas fried slowly in butter*	aine sauté ti pois. *an soh-tay tee pwa.*
Je voudrais ... *I would like ...*	Mo oulé ... *Moh hoo-lay*
du café noir *black coffee*	café sans di lait *kah-fay san dee-lay*
du café au lait *white coffee*	café avec di lait *kah-fay ah-vek dee-lay*
du vin *wine*	di vin *deev-hein*
une glace à la vanille *vanilla ice-cream*	ène sorbet la vanille *an sore-bay lah-vah-nee*
du fromage *cheese*	fromaze *fromazz*
un dessert *a dessert*	aine dessert *an day-sair*
L'addition, s'il vous plaît! *The bill, please.*	Bill/Addition s'il vous plaît. *Bill seel-voo-play.*
Est-ce que le service est compris? *Is service included?*	Service compris? *Sair-veess lah-dan?*
Pas de pourboires. *No tips*	Pas éna pourboire. *Pas hay-nay poor-bwar.*

Quelques indications sur la cuisine mauricienne

La Cuisine Créole

Le curry

C'est une sauce contenant du piment et d'autres épices tels que le safran, le coriandre, le gingembre, le poivre et l'ail. On peut mettre dans cette sauce, de la viande, du poisson ou des légumes. On mange le tout avec du riz ou du pain.

Le rôti de langue de boeuf

On fait rôtir la langue de boeuf après l'avoir fait bouillir et l'avoir injectée d'épices tels que l'ail, le gingembre, le poivre, la cannelle, le girofle, le siaw et l'ajinomoto. On y ajoute aussi un peu de miel.
Le porc rôti et le poulet sont aussi très appréciés.

La Rougaille

C'est une sauce rouge épicée à l'ail, au gingembre et au poivre, avec un peu de thym, de persil et d'ajinomoto. L'élément de base de la rougaille est la pomme d'amour, variété de tomate. Dans cette sauce on peut aussi mettre de la viande, du corned beef, des saucisses, du poisson, du poisson salé, de la viande salée ou même du bombli.

Les grains secs

Les grains secs accompagnent souvent les currys ou les rougailles. Il y a une grande variété de ces grains tels que les lentilles noires ou rouges, le dholl, les haricots blancs ou rouges ou pâles, les gros pois, les petits pois verts ou jaunes et les embrevades. Ces grains sont souvent préparés en fricassée.

Les fricassées de légumes

Beaucoup de légumes peuvent être utilisés, par exemple, des bringelles (aubergines), le chouchou, le giraumon, le chou, les lalos, les margozes, les pipengailles. Ces légumes sont préparés avec du thym, du persil, du poivre, des oignons, de l'ail, du gingembre, un peu d'ajinomoto et une ou deux pommes d'amour. On peut y ajouter un peu de viande salée, ou de lard ou de bacon.

Des brèdes à l'étouffée

Ce sont des brèdes qu'on fait cuire à la vapeur avec un peu de poivre, d'ajinomoto, d'ail, de gingembre et d'oignon haché finement. On y ajoute parfois un peu de viande salée, de bacon ou du lard.

Les bouillons de brèdes

Ce sont des brèdes qu'on fait cuire en bouillon avec un peu d'oignon, d'ail et de gingembre écrasés, du poivre et d'ajinomoto. Ces bouillons accompagnent souvent un curry assez fort ou une rougaille épicée avec un plat de riz.
Il y a toute une variété de brèdes : brède mouroume, brède martin, brède malbar, brède de chine, brède cresson, brède giraumon, brède chouchou.
Un bouillon peut aussi se faire avec du poisson et des margoze, ou du poisson salé, ou avec le tec-tec (un petit mollusque) ou avec des bigorneaux (des coquillages comestibles).

Le Vindaye

C'est une sauce très épicée préparée avec de l'ail et du gingembre, du safran, de petits oignons, de gros piments, du vinaigre et de l'huile de moutarde. Dans la sauce on peut mettre du poisson ou des ourites (des pieuvres). On mange le vindaye avec du riz ou du pain.

La Cuisine Chinoise

Les bouillons

II y a une variété de bouillons tels que le bouillon de crabe, le bouillon van-yen (des boulettes de poisson), le bouillon mee foon (un genre de vermicelle à base de riz) dans lequel on met des pousses de bambou, des champignons chinois, des oeuf au plat et du poulet.
La Soupe Mama est préparée avec du filet de poisson, du riz, un peu de brandy, d'huile d'olive, de gingembre haché, d'ajinomoto, des oeufs et le bouillon est fait avec une tête de poisson.

Les oeufs rôtis à la chinoise

On fait rôtir ces oeufs avec du siaw, un peu d'huile et d'eau, du vin rouge, un peu de "riz rouge" (siouk), d'anis étoile et de poudre de Heung Neu Fun (les 5 épices). Ces oeufs sont servis avec une sauce d'ail et de la salade.

Le poisson aigre-doux

C'est du poisson accompagné d'une sauce préparée avec des légumes (de petites carottes, un petit concombre tendre et de petits chouchoux bien verts), du gingembre, de la poudre *cange (*de l'amidon en poudre), du poivre, un peu d'ajinomoto, du sucre blanc et du vinaigre blanc. Le plat est décoré avec un peu de mee-foon passé à l'huile, des feuilles de laitue et des rondelles de tomate.

Poulet aux trois merveilles

C'est du poulet accompagné d'une sauce préparée avec des légumes (des champignons "Tong ku", des champignons "Oreilles" et des pousses de bambou), du siaw, de la poudre *cange*, du vin rouge et un peu d'ajinomoto. Ce plat est servi avec du riz.

Le Mee-Foon

Ce sont des nouilles frites préparées avec du poulet, des queues d'oignon, et des oeufs.

Le riz frit ou riz cantonnais

C'est du riz frit dans lequel on peut mettre de la viande de boeuf, de la volaille, des saucisses ou du poisson frit, des oeufs, le tout préparé avec du siaw et des queues d'oignon.

Le Foo-Yung

C'est une omelette chinoise préparée avec des crustacés ou du poulet, des champignons, des carottes, des pousses de petits pois, des oignons, du poivre, de l'ajinomoto, un peu de sucre et du rhum blanc.

Le Bol Renversé

C'est du riz préparé avec du boeuf ou du poulet, des saucisses chinoises, du porc, des champignons, des épices et du vin rouge.

La Cuisine Indienne et Musulmane

Le Briani

C'est un plat de riz épicé dans lequel on peut mettre du cabri, du boeuf, du cerf, du poulet ou du poisson. Le riz est préparé avec des épices comme de l'ail, du gingembre, du safran oriental, du cerfeuil, de la menthe, du cumin, de la cannelle. On y met aussi des pommes de terre, du *mantègue* (beurre clarifié) et du lait caillé.

Le Moulougtany

C'est une soupe épicée qu'on prépare avec du poulet, des crustacés, du dholl, des aubergines et des brèdes songe.
C'est un plat de riz préparé avec des morceaux de poulet, des oignons, des épices tels que l'ail, le gingembre, des piments rouges, de la poudre à cari et du safran.

Le Kat-Lesse

C'est une pâte, comme un tourne-dos/burger préparée avec de la viande hachée, des queues d'oignons, des oignons, des oeufs, de la chapelure et du cumin, qu'on fait frire, le tout servi avec de la salade.

Les Achards de légumes

Ce sont des légumes émincés qu'on fait saler et sécher avant de les mélanger dans une sauce préparée avec de la moutarde, du safran, des piments verts, des oignons, et du vinaigre. Les légumes qui s'y prêtent sont le choufleur, le chou, les haricots verts et les carottes.

A few hints on the Mauritian Cuisine

The Créole Cuisine

The Curry

This is a sauce made up of chilli and other spices namely turmeric, coriander, ginger, pepper and garlic. It goes with meat, fish and vegetables alike, and the whole can be eaten with either rice or bread.

Roast Ox Tongue

First the ox tongue is boiled, then punched all over and stuffed with spices like garlic, ginger, pepper, cinnamon, and clove. It is also injected with ajinomoto dissolved in soy sauce. A little honey is added, after which the whole thing is left to roast.
Roast pork and roast chicken are likewise very popular.

The 'Rougaille'

This is a spicy red sauce containing garlic, ginger and pepper as well as thyme, parsley and ajinomoto. *"Love-apple"*, a variety of tomato, is the main ingredient. Meat, corned beef, sausages, fish, salt-fish, salt-meat and even *'bomli'*: bombay duck (a type of thin fish) can all fit in.

Dry Grains

Dry grains often accompany curries or 'rougailles'. There is a large variety of them namely black or red lentils, dholl, white or red or pale kidney beans, butter beans, green or yellow peas as well as pigeon peas. They are normally cooked into a stew.

Stewed vegetables

A lot of vegetables can be cooked in this way : aubergine, chow-chow red pumpkin, cabbage, lady's fingers, bitter gourds, sponge gourd! etc. These are relished with thyme, parsley, pepper, onions, garlic ginger, a little ajinomoto and a couple of tomatoes. Salt meat or bacon can also be added.

Stewed Leaves

The leaves are made to stew dressed with a little pepper, ajinomoto, garlic, ginger and minced onion. Salt-meat or bacon can also fit in.

Leaf broths or boiled leaves

These are leaves boiled in water with a little onion, pounded garlic and ginger, pepper and ajinomoto. Such broths often pair with a rather tangy curry or a spicy 'rougaille' taken with rice. There is a whole range of edible leaves: drum stick leaves, morel, 'malbar', Indian mustard, water cress, pumpkin leaves, chowchow leaves etc.
Broths can also be prepared with fish and bitter gourds, salt-fish, 'tec-tec' (a mollusc), and winkies (edible shell-fish).

The 'Vindaye'

This is a very spicy sauce prepared with garlic, ginger, turmeric, onions, vinegar and mustard oil. Fish or octopuses are then left to soak in it. The 'vindaye' can be eaten with both rice and bread.

The Chinese Cuisine

Broths

A whole variety of broths exists namely crab broth, van-yen broth (with fish balls), mee foon broth (which includes a kind of vermicelli prepared with rice, bamboo shoots, Chinese mushrooms, fried eggs and chicken). The Mama Soup is prepared with fillets of fish, rice, a little brandy, olive oil, minced ginger, ajinomoto and eggs while the broth itself is made with a fish head.

Chinese roast eggs

These are eggs roasted in a mixture of soy sauce, a little oil and water, red wine, a little 'red rice' (siouk), Chinese anise, and Heung New Fun powder (the five spices). They are then served with a sauce of garlic and salad.

The sweet-sour fish preparation

This consists of fish in a sauce made up of vegetables—small carrots, a small tender cucumber and very fresh small chochoes – ginger, starch powder, pepper, a little ajinomoto, white sugar a vinegar. The dish is decorated with a little mee-foon, lettuce leaves and a few tomato rings.

The 'Poulet aux trois Merveilles'

This is a chicken dish in a sauce which consists of vegetables ('Tong ku' mushrooms, 'ear' mushrooms, and bamboo shoots), soy sauce, starch powder, red wine and a little ajinomoto. The dish is served with rice.

The 'Mee-Foon'

This is fried noodles prepared with chicken, onion stalks and eggs.

Fried Rice

This dish consists of fried rice with either beef, chicken, sausages or fried fish, together with eggs. Soy sauce and onion stalks also into the preparation.

The 'Foo-Yung'

This is a Chinese omelet prepared with crustacea or mushrooms, carrots, green-pea sprouts, onion, pepper, ajinomoto, a little sugar and white rum.

The 'Bol Renversé'

This consists of rice prepared with beef or chicken, Chinese sausages, pork, mushrooms, spices and red wine.

The Indian and Muslim Cuisine

The Biryani

This is a spicy rice dish with goat meat, beef, deer meat, chicken, or fish. The rice is mixed with spices like garlic, ginger, *jaffrane* : saffron, chervil, mint, cumin and cinnamon. Potatoes, ghee and curd also go into the mixture.

The 'Vendillon' Curry

This is a very spicy curry prepared with curry powder (massala), tamarind, onions, aubergines, garlic, fenugreek and chilli. You can also have it with *'bombli'*.

The 'Kaliah'

It is a very spicy sauce with either goat-meat, beef, mutton or deer-meat, chicken, fish and potatoes. It is prepared with spices, ghee and curd.

The 'Kutcha'

This is a kind of pickles with grated green mangoes or cythera fruits.

The Tandouri Chicken'

This is chicken soaked in curd and in a dough of curry powder with red dye before it is baked. It is served with salads and 'faratas'.

The 'Vindalloo Chicken'

This is a very spicy dish served with rice and prepared with cumin, mustard seeds, turmeric, black pepper, ginger, cinnamon, garlic, red chilli and white vinegar.

The 'Halim'

This is a soup prepared with chicken/goat-meat, dholl, pounded wheat, spices and chilli. It is served with bread.

The 'Moulougtany'

This is a spicy soup prepared with chicken, crustacea, dholl, aubergines and dasheen leaves.

The 'Pilau'

This is a rice dish with pieces of chicken, onions, spices like garlic, ginger, red chilli, curry powder and turmeric.

The 'Kat-Lesse'

This is a burger made of mince meat with green onions, onions, spices like garlic, ginger, curry powder, turmeric, bread crumbs and beaten eggs.

Vegetable Pickles

These are salted vegetables thinly sliced which are left to dry for some time before being mixed with a sauce of turmeric, green chilli, onions and vinegar. The vegetables mostly used are cauliflower, cabbage, French beans and carrots.

Au marché/At the market

French	Creole
Donnez-moi un demi-kilo … *Give me half a kilo …*	Donne moi aine démi kilo … *Donn mwa an day-mee kilo …*
de viande *of meat*	la vianne *lah viann*
de poisson *of fish*	poisson *pwah-sson*
de morue *of cod*	la mori *lah moh-ree*
de boeuf *of beef*	bèfe *beff*
d'aubergines *of aubergines*	brinzelle *brein-zell*
de champignons *of mushrooms*	sampion *samp-ee-on*
de citrouille *of pumpkin*	ziromon *zee-roh-mon*
de poireaux *of leeks*	poireaux *pwar-ro*
de haricots verts *of French beans*	zaricot vert *zah-ree-co vair*
de piments verts/rouges *of green/red chilli*	pima verts/rouze *pee-mah vair/rooze*
de patates douces *sweet potatoes*	patates *pah-tatt*
de pistaches *peanuts*	pisse-tasse *piss-tass*
d'onions *of onions*	zonion *zoh-nee-on*
de tomates *of tomatoes*	pomme d'amour *pomm-dahmoor*
d'épinard *of spinach (greens)*	zépinar *zay-pee-nar*

French / English	Creole / Pronunciation
Je voudrais … *I would like …*	Mou oulé *Moh hoo-lay …*
une langue de boeuf *an ox tongue*	aine la langue bèfe *an lah lang beff*
un poulet *a chicken*	aine poulet *an poo-lay*
un chou-fleur *a cauliflower*	aine li sou-flère *an lee soo-flair*
deux pâtissons *two squash-melons*	dé patisson *day pat-tee-sson*
un ananas *a pineapple*	aine zanana *an zah-nah-nah*
une noix de coco *a coconut*	aine coco *an coco*
deux cents letchis *two hundred litchis*	dé cents letchis *day san let-see*
dix mangues *ten mangoes*	disse mangues *diss mangg*
une poire et une pomme *a pear and an apple*	aine poire ek aine pomme *an pwar ek an pomm*
trois oranges *three oranges*	trois zoranges *trwah zoh-ranz*
une main de bananes *a bunch of bananas*	aine la mé bananes *an lah may bann-hann*
une pastèque *a water melon*	aine moulon d'eau *an moo-lon-doh*
un bouquet de persil *a bunch of parsley*	aine paquet persil *an pac-kay pair-see*
une botte de radis *a bunch of radishes*	aine paquet radis *an pac-kay rah-dee*
une salade de laitue *a lettuce*	aine salade laitie *an salad lay-tee*
demi-kilo d'ail/une live d'ail *half a kilo of garlic/a pound of garlic*	démi kilo l'ail/aine live l'ail *day-mee kilo lah-*yee/an *leave lah-yee*

French / English	Creole / Pronunciation
Pesez … pour moi, s'il vous plaît *Weigh … for me, please*	Pèse … pou moi, s'il vous plaît. *Pays … poo mwah, seel-voo play*
ce poisson *this fish*	sa poisson la *sah pwah-sson lah*
ce crabe *this crab*	sa crabe la *sah crab lah*
ce homard *this lobster*	sa homard la *sah ho-mar lah*
cette poule *this hen*	sa poule la *sah pool lah*
cette pieuvre *this octopus*	sa ourite lah *sah hoo-ritt lah*
Donnez-moi … *Give me …*	Donne moi … *Donn mwah …*
deux paires de dholl puri *two pairs of 'dhollpourri'*	dé paire dal pourri *day pair dall poo-ree*
une paire de rôti *a pair of 'roti'*	aine paire rôti *an pair roh-tee*
dix gâteaux piments *ten 'chilli-cakes'*	disse gâteaux pima *diss gah-toh pee-mah*
cinq samoussas *five 'samoussas'*	cinq samoussa *sank sah-moo-sah*
un verre d'alouda *a glass of 'alouda'*	aine verre alouda *an vair ha-loo-dah*
un verre de lait à la vanille *a glass of milk with vanilla*	aine verre dilé la vani *an vair dee-lay vah-nee*
un pain avec du achard de légumes *a loaf with vegetables pickles*	aine dipin avec zassar légumes *an dee-pein ha-vek zah-sar leg-him*
une portion de frites *a portion of chips*	aine portion frites *an por-see-on fritt*
un pain avec du vindaye *a loaf with 'vindaye'*	aine dipin avec vindaye *an dee-pein ha-vek veen-dah-yee*

French	Creole
un croissant *a crescent roll*	aine croissant *an crwass-san*
une baguette *a French stick*	aine baguette *an bag-get*
un pain maison *a cottage loaf*	aine dipin maison *an dee-pain may-zon*
une brioche *a small milk loaf bun*	aine briosse *an bree-oss*

C'est combien …?
How much is …?

Comié …?
Ko-mee-yeah …?

French	Creole
cette longue robe *this long dress*	sa longue robe la *sah long rob lah*
cette longue jupe *this long skirt*	sa longue zippe la *sah long zip lah*
ce T-Shirt *this T-Shirt*	sa T-Shirt la *sah T-Shirt lah*
ce chemisier *this lady's blouse*	sa blouse la *sah blooz lah*
ce jean *this pair of jeans*	sa jean la *sah jean lah*
ce pantalon *this pair of trousers*	sa canne-son la *sah cann-son lah*
ce short *this pair of shorts*	sa short la *sah short lah*
ce caftan *this caftan*	sa caftan la *sah kaff-tan lah*
ce chapeau de paille *this straw hat*	sa sapo la paille la *sah sah-poh lah pah-yee lah*
cette casquette *this cap*	sa casquette la *sah kass-ket lah*
ce paréo *this 'pareo'*	sa paréo lah *sah pah-ray-ho lah*
cette pair de 'savates' en caoutchouc *this pair of rubber flip-flops*	sa paire savate caoutchou la *sah pair sah-vat ka-hoot-soo lah*

Le transport/Transport

Quoi dire/what to say

Où se trouve …? *Where is …?*	Cotte …? *Kot …?*
la station de taxis *the taxi stand*	la place taxi *lah plass taxi*
la gare d'autobus *the bus station*	la gare bisse *lah gar biss*
Où puis-je trouver …? *Where can I get …?*	Cotte mo capave trouve …? *Kot moh kah-pave troov …?*
un taxi *a taxi*	aine taxi *an taxi*
une agence de location de voitures *a rent-a-car service agency*	aine lazence ki loué loto *an lah-zennss kee loo-way loh-toh.*
Conduisez-moi à l'hôtel … *Take me to the hotel …*	Amène moi lotel … *Ah-men mwa loh-tell …*
Conduisez-moi à cette adresse *Drive me to this address.*	Amène moi sa l'adresse la. *Ah-men mwah sah lah-dress lah.*
Je suis pressé. *I'm in a hurry.*	Mo pressé *Moh pray-say.*
D'où part l'autobus de (Port Louis)? *Where does the bus for (Port Louis) leave from?*	Cotte bisse démaré Port Louis? *Kot biss day-may-ray Port Louis?*
A quelle heure part le prochain bus? *At what time will the next bus leave?*	Quand lote bisse allé? *Kan lot biss ah-lay?*
Est-ce le bus de Curepipe? *Is it the bus to Curepipe?*	Sa bisse la alle Curepipe? *Sah biss lah hal Keer-peep?*

A quelle heure l'autobus arrive-t-il au centre ville? *At what time does the bus reach the town centre?*	Qui lère bisse vine dans sante la ville? *Kee lair biss veen dan sant lah-veel?*
C'est combien le ticket d'autobus? *What is the bus fare?*	Comié tickette la couté? *Ko-me-yeah ticket lah koo-tay?*
Monsieur le receveur, s'il vous plaît? *Conductor please?*	Controlère s'il vous plaît? *Kon-tro-lair seel-voo-play?*
Je n'ai pas de monnaie. *I haven't got any change.*	Mo pas éna casse sanzé. *Moh pay-nah kass san-zay.*
Vous ne m'avez pas rendu la monnaie. *You haven't given me any change.*	Ou pas fine ranne moi casse. *Hoo pah fine ranne moi casse.*
Le contrôleur — Sortez vos tickets! *The ticket-collector — Please show your tickets!*	Tchaike — Montré tickette! Check — *mon-tray ticket!*
Faut-il changer d'autobus? *Do we have to change buses?*	Bizin sanze bisse? *Bee-zein sanz biss?*
Pouvez-vous me dire où je dois descendre? *Can you tell me where to get down please?*	Ou capave dire moi cotte pou dessanne? *Hoo kah-pav deer mwa kot poo day-sann?*
Arrêtez-moi à l'arrêt le plus proche *Leave me at the nearest bus stop.*	Arrête-moi biss stop pli pré. *Ah-rett mwa biss-stop plee pray.*
Je vous dois combien? *How much do I owe you?*	Comié mo doit ou? *Ko-me-yeah moh dwa hoo?*
Combien je vous dois pour la course? *What's your fare?*	Comié mo doit où pou sa course la? *Ko-me-yeah poo sah coorss lah?*
Attendez-moi ici. Je reviens dans dix minutes. *Wait for me here. I'll be back in ten minutes.*	Attane moi ici. Mo vini dans disse minites. *Ah-tann mwah hee-see. Moh vee-nee dan diss mee-neet.*

French	Creole
Comment vous contacter? *How to reach you?*	Ki manière pou contacté où? *Kee mah-nee-air poo kon-tac-tay hoo?*
Laissez-moi vos coordonnés. *Leave me your reference.*	Laisse ou référence. *Layss hoo ray-fay-ranss.*
Puis-je louer une voiture …? *Can I hire a car …?*	Mo capave loué aine loto …? *Moh kapav loo-hay hen loh-toh …?*
pour cinq personnes *for five persons*	pou cinq dimounes *poo sank dee-moon*
pour une semaine *for a week*	pou aine sémaine *poo an say-men*
pour le week-end *for the week-end*	pou week-end *poo week-end*
décapotable *convertible*	décapotable *day-kah-poh-tab*
J'ai besoin d'une voiture. *I need a car.*	Mo bizin aine loto. *Moh bee-zein an loh-toh.*
J'ai été bloqué dans un embouteillage. *I was taken up in a traffic jam.*	Mo fine tassé dans trafic. *Moh feen tah-say dan trafik.*
Combien dois-je payer? *How much do I have to pay?*	Comié mo bizin payé? *Ko-me-yeah moh bees-hein pay-yeah?*
Puis-je payer par chèque? *May I pay by cheque?*	Mo capave paye par chèque? *Moh kapav payee par check?*
Quels sont les papiers qu'il me faut? *What papers that are needed?*	Qui papier mo bizin? *Kee pah-pee-yeah moh bees-hein?*
Il y a-t-il des arrhes à verser? *Need I make any deposit?*	Bizin laisse avaloir? *Bees-hein layss ha-vah-loh-are?*
Quel est le tarif …? *What is the charge …?*	Ki so tarif…? *Kee soh tah-reef?*
au kilomètre *per kilometre*	par kilomètre *par kee-loh-met*
à la journée *per day*	pou la zourné *poo lah zoor-nay*

Je pense que la batterie est morte. *I think that the battery is dead.*	Mo croire ki batterie fine désarzé. *Moh kro-are kee battery feen day-sar-zay.*
Quel est le montant de l'assurance? *What is the cost of insurance?*	Qui prix l'assirance? *Kee pree lah-see-ranss?*
En cas d'ennuis, que dois-je faire? *In case of trouble, what must I do?*	Si mo gagne problème, qui mo pou bizin faire? *See moh gah-ee problem, kee moh beez-hen fair?*
En cas de panne, qui est responsable des réparations? *In case of breakdown, who is responsible for the repairs?*	Si mo gagne panne, qui sanne-là capave dépanne-moi? *See moh ga-hee pann, kee sann-lah ka-pav day-pann mwa?*
Je suis tombé en panne. *I've got a breakdown.*	Mo fine tomme en panne. *Moh feen tomm han pann.*
J'ai eu un accident. *I've had an accident.*	Mo fine faire ène accident. *Moh feen fair an accidan.*
Où se trouve la station service? *Where is the filling-station?*	Cotte filling été. *Kot filling hay-tay?*
Faites le plein s'il vous plaît. *Fill up the tank please.*	Rempli tank s'il vous plaît. *Remp-lee tank seel-voo-play.*
Vérifiez ... *Check ...*	Tchaik *Check*
la batterie *the battery*	batterie *battery*
le niveau de l'huile *the oil*	di l'huile *deel-wheel*
les bougies *the spark plugs*	la bougie *lah bouze-hee*
la pression des pneus *the tyre pressure*	pression la roue *pray-see-on lah roo*

Je dois aller chez le garagiste. *I must go to the mechanic.*	Mo bizin alle guette aine mécanicien. *Moh beez-hein hal gate/gait an may-kah-nee-see-hein.*
Je dois faire réparer ... *I must get the ..... repaired*	Mo bizin faire répare ... *Moh beez-hen faire ray-par*
les freins *brakes*	freins *fr-hein*
l'échappement *exhaust*	l'essapement *lay-sapp-man*
le pare-choc *bumper*	paresoc *par-sok*
le klaxon *horn*	trompe *tromp*
J'ai des problèmes pour démarrer. *I've got problems to start the car.*	Mo éna problème pour démarrer. *Moh hay-nah problem pou day-mah-ray.*
Combien je vous dois ? *How much do I have to pay?*	Comié mo bizin payé? *Ko-me-yeah moh bees-hein pay-yeah?*
Il me faut ... *I need a ...*	Mo bizin ... *Mo beez-hein ...*
un écrou *nut*	aine zécrou *an zay-kroo*
un cric *jack*	aine verrin *an vay-rhein*
un pneu *tyre*	aine la roue *an lah roo*
Le jour de mon départ, puis-je laisser la voiture à l'aéroport? *On the day of my departure, may I leave my car at the airport?*	Zour mo allé, eski mo capave laisse loto aire-porte? *Zoor moh ha-lay, esse-kee moh ka-pav layss loh-toh airport?*
A qui remette les clés? *To whom shall I return the keys?*	Are ki sanne-là mo ranne la clé? *Are kee sann-lah moh rann la clay?*

Réactions probables/Likely reactions

Complet *Full up*	Rempli *Ram-plee*
Entrez! *Come in!*	Entrez *Han-tray*
Descendez! *Get down!*	Dessanne *Day-sann*
Dépêchez-vous! *Hurry-up!*	Dégazé *Day-gah-zay.*
J'arrive. *I'm coming.*	Mo vini. *Moh vee-nee.*
Changez d'autobus à (Curepipe). *Change bus at Curepipe.*	Sanze biss Kirpipe. *Sanz biss Keer-peep.*
Voici votre arrêt. *This is your stop.*	Ou dessanne ici. *Hoo day-sann hee-see.*
Vous me devez trente roupies. *You owe me thirty rupees.*	Ou doit moi trente roupies. *Hoo dwa mwa trant roo-pee.*
Vous descendez au prochain arrêt. *You'll get down at the next stop.*	Ou dessanne lotte bisse-stop. *Hoo day-sann lot biss stop.*
Vous pouvez m'appeler chez moi. *You can phone me at my place.*	Ou capave téléphone-moi cotte moi. *Hoo ka-pav tay-lay-fon mwa kot mwa.*
Je n'ai plus de voitures disponibles. *There's no car available.*	Mo né pli éna loto libe. *Moh nay plee hay-nah loh-toh leeb.*
Donnez-moi votre permis de conduire. *Let me have your driving licence.*	Donne moi ou licence. *Don mwa hoo licence.*
Si vous tombez en panne, adressez-vous au … *In case of breakdown, contact …*	Si ou gagne panne, contacté … *See hoo ga-hee pann, kon-tack-tay…*
Laissez les clés chez … *Leave the keys with …*	Laisse la clé cotte … *Layss lah clay kot …*

J'ai laissé les clés de la voiture dans ma chambre. *I've left the keys of the car in my room.*	Mo fine laisse la clé l'auto dans mo la samme. *Moh feen layss lah clay loh-toh dan moh lah sam.*

À LA POSTE/AT THE POST OFFICE

Quoi dire/What to say

Je voudrais … *I'd like …*	Mo oulé … *Moh hoo-lay …*
faire un appel à l'étranger *to place an external phone call*	téléphone lotte pays *tay-lay fon lot pay-yee*
envoyer un télégramme *to send a telegram*	envoye aine télégramme *han-voy an tay-lay-gram*
faire recommander une lettre *to have a letter registered*	enrézistré aine lettre *han-ray-ziss-tray an let*
envoyer un colis-postal … *to send a parcel-post …*	envoye aine parcel par la poste *han-voy an parcel par lah post*
des timbres *to have some stamps*	impé taime *hein-pay temm*
un timbre à dix roupies *to have a ten-rupee stamp*	aine taime disse roupies *an temm diss roo-pee*
un aérogramme *to have an air-letter*	aine air laitte-hère *an air letter*
C'est pour … *It's for …*	Mo oulé … *Moh hoo-lay …*
affranchir une lettre *posting a letter*	posté aine laitte *poss-tay enn let*
un envoi d'argent *a remittance*	envoye larzan *han-voy lar-zan*
un mandat-poste *a post-office/postal order*	aine mandat-poste *an man-dah post.*

French	Creole
C'est combien une lettre? …	Combien couté pou envoye aine laitte …?
What's the postage fee of a letter …?	*Koh-mee-yeah koo-tay poo han-voy an let …?*
pour l'Angleterre *to England*	pou l'Angleterre *poo Lang-lay-tair*
pour la France *to France*	pou la France *poo lah Franss*
pour la Réunion *to Réunion*	pou la Réunion *poo lah Ray-nee-on*
pour les Seychelles *to Seychelles*	pou Seychelles *poo Say-shell*
pour Madagascar *to Madagascar*	pou Madagascar *poo Mah-dah-gas-car*
C'est combien …? *What's the postage fee of …*	Comié payé pou …? *Koh-mee-yeah pay-yeah poo …?*
un colis par avion *a parcel by air mail*	aine parcel par avion *an parcel par ah-vee-on*
une lettre ordinaire *a letter by surface mail*	aine laitte ordinaire *an let or-dee-nair*
A quelle heure se fait …? *What's the time of …?*	Qui lère …? *Kee lair …?*
la levée des lettres *the collection of letters*	collecté laitte *collect-tay let*
la distribution des lettres *the delivery of letters*	délivré laitte *day-lee-vray let*
Quel est le côut de la lettre?	Comié sa lette la couté pou avoyé?
What's the postage fee of the letter?	*Koh-mee-yeah sah let lah koo-tay poo ah-vo-yeah?*
Quel est le tarif? *What is the rate?*	Qui so tarif? *Kee soh tariff?*
Y a-t-il une surcharge à payer? *Is there any surchage to pay?*	Ena larzan en plisse pou payé? *Hay-nah lar-zan han pliss poo pay-yeah?*

Réactions probables/Likely reactions

Donnez-moi votre numéro *Let me have your number.*	Donne moi ou niméro. *Donn mwa hoo nee-may-roh.*
Il vous faut attendre pour *You'll have to wait before*	Ou bizin attanne pou *Hoo bees-hein hat-tann poo*
entrer en communication *being put through to …*	rentre han comminication avec … *rant han koh-mee-nee-kah-see-on ah-vek*
Cabine téléphonique numéro (deux) *Telephone box number (two)*	Cabine téléphonique niméro (dé) *Cabin tay-lay-pho-nik nee-may-roh (day).*
Il y a une attente/un retard. *There's a delay*	Ena aine rétard. *Hay-nah an ray-tar.*
Laisse-moi essayer à nouveau. *Let me try again*	Laisse mo séyé encor. *Less mo say-yeah han-kor.*
Ne quittez pas *Hold on*	Pas quitté *Pah kit-tay*
Vous êtes en ligne *You are through*	Ou lor la ligne *Hoo law lah leen*
Parlez *Speak*	Causé *Koh-zay*
Ne coupez pas *Hold on/hold the line*	Pas coupé *Pah koo-pay*
La ligne est en dérangement *The line is out of order*	La ligne pas marsé *Lah leen pah mar-say*
La ligne est occupée *The line is engaged*	La ligne engagé *Lah leen han-gay-zay*
Remplissez ce formulaire. *Fill in this form.*	Rempli sa forme la. *Rem-plee sah form lah.*

Signez ici. *Sign here.*	Signe ici. *See-gne hee-see.*
Pas de distribution le dimanche *No delivery on Sundays.*	Laitte pas délivré dimansse. *Let pah day-lee-vray dee-manss.*
Faites peser la lettre. *Have the letter weighed.*	Faire pèse ou laitte. *Fair pays hoo let.*
Vous avez oublié de cacheter la lettre. *You've forgotten to seal the letter.*	Ou fine blié ferme ou laite. *Hoo finn blee-yeah fairm hoo let.*
Mettez ici l'adresse du destinataire. *Write down here the receiver's address.*	Mette ladresse destinataire ici. *Mett lah-drayss dayss-tee-nah-tair he-see.*

Quoi dire/What to say

C'est combien …? *How much is/are …?*	Comié …? *Koh-mee-yeah …?*
ce maillot de bain *this bathing suit*	sa maillot la *sah mah-yee-ho lah*
ce bikini *this bikini*	sa bikini la *sah bikini la*
cette salopette *these dungarees*	sa salopette la *sah sah-loh-pet lah*
ces sandales *these sandals*	sa sandalette la *sah sand-ha-let lah*
ces nu-pieds *these beach-shoes*	sa soulier la plaze la *sah soo-lee-yeah lah plaz lah*
ce parasol *this umbrella*	sa parasol la *sah pah-rah-sol lah*
ce bonnet de bain *this swimming cap*	sa bonnet de bain la *sah boh-nay-day ben lah*
cette veste *this jacket*	sa jackette la *sah jacket lah*
cette chemise de nuit *this nightdress*	sa robe de chambre la *sah rob day samb lah*
cet imperméable *this raincoat*	sa pardessus la *sah par-day-see lah*
ce sac en toile *this canvas bag*	sa sac la toile la *sah sack lah twal lah*
cette petite tente en raffia *this small raffia bag*	sa ti tente rafia la *sah tee tant rah-fee-ha-lah*
Je voudrais … *May I have …*	Mo oulé … *Moh hoo-lay …*
une pelle pour la plage *a beach shovel*	aine la pelle pou la plaze *enn lah-pel poo lah plaz*

quelque chose comme ça *something like this*	kiksoze coume sa *kick-soz coom sah*
un seau pour la plage *a beach bucket*	aine séau pou la plaze *enn say-ho poo lah plaz*
un comme ça *one like this*	aine coume sa *enn coom sah*
un ballon pour la plage *a beach ball*	aine boule pou la plaze *enn bool poo lah plaz*
un scaphandre *a diving-suit*	aine combinaison pou plonzé *enn comb-ee-nay-zon poo plon-zay*
un parasol pour la plage *a beach umbrella*	aine parasol pou la plaze *hen pah-rah-sol poo lah plaz*
des palmes *flippers*	la patte canard *lah pat ka-nar*
des lunettes de soleil *sunglasses*	linette soleil *lee-net soh-lay-ee*
une raquette *a racket*	aine raquette *an racket*
une valise *a suitcase*	aine valise *an vah-leeze*
une canne à pêche *a fishing rod*	aine la ligne pou la pesse *an lah lee-gne poo lah payss*

Avez-vous ...? *Do you have ...?*	Ou éna ...? *Hoo hay-nay ...?*
des chaussures en cuir *leather shoes*	souliers en cuir/la peau *soo-lee-yeah-han kweer/ lah po*
des chaussures en toile *canvas shoes*	soulier la toile *soo-lee-yeah lah twal*
des tissus en nylon *nylon material*	tissi nylon *tee-see nee-lon*
des tissus en coton *cotton fabric*	tissi coton *tee-see coton*
des tissus à fleurs *flowered material*	tissi à flère *tee-see-ha flair*

French	Creole
Où puis-je trouver …? *Where can I find …?*	Cotte mo capave trouve …? *Kot moh kah-pav troov …?*
cela *this*	sa *sah*
des disques *records*	ban disques *bann disc*
des cassettes *cassettes/tapes*	cassette *cassette.*
Je peux l'essayer? *May I try it on?*	Mo capave seye li? *Moh kah-pav say-yee lee?*
Mon numéro, c'est le … *My size is …*	Mo niméro …/Mo mette taille… *Moh nee-may-roh…/Moh met tie…*
C'est … *It's …*	Li … *Lee …*
trop grand *too big/large*	trop grand *tro gran*
trop petit *too small*	trop piti *trop pee-tee*
bien *O.K/all right*	bon *ok*
Ça me va. *It suits/fits me.*	Li bon. *Lee correck.*
Je le prends. *I'm taking it.*	Mo prend li. *Moh pran lee.*
Avez-vous quelque chose …? *Have you got anything …?*	Ou éna kiksoze …? *Hoo hay-na kick-soze …?*
comme ça *like this*	coume sa *coom sah*
de plus grand *bigger*	pli grand *plee gran*
de moins cher *cheaper*	moins sère *mwen sair*
de plus petit *smaller*	pli piti *plee pee-tee*
de différent *different*	différent *dee-fay-ran.*

Je regarde simplement. *I'm just browsing.*	Mo pé zisse guetté. *Moh pay ziss gay-tay.*
Merci bien. *Thank you very much.*	Merci. *Mair-see.*
Est-ce que vous faites une remise? *Is there a discount?*	Ou pou faire rédiction? *Hoo poo fair ray-dick-see-on?*
Pouvez-vous m'aider? *Can you help me?*	Ou capave aide moi? *Koo kah-pav aid mwa?*
Vous acceptez des chèques? *Do you accept cheques?*	Ou accepté chèque? *Hoo hack-sep-tay seck?*
Je peux payer par chèque? *May I pay by cheque?*	Mo capave paie par chèque? *Moh kah-pav payee par seck?*
Vous ouvrez/fermez à quelle heure? *At what time do you open/close?*	Ou ouvert/fermé qui lère? *Hoo hoo-vair/fermay kee lair?*
Le reçu s'il vous plaît. *The receipt, please.*	Aine réssi s'il vous plaît. *An ray-see seel-voo-play.*

Réactions probables/Likely reactions

Vous désirez quelque chose? *Can I help you?*	Ou bizin kiksoze? *Hoo bees-hein kick-soze?*
Ça c'est … *This one is …*	Ça … *Sah …*
Je peux vous aider? *Is there anything I can do for you?*	Mo capave aide ou? *Moh kah-pav head hoo?*
Vous désirez autre chose? *Do you want anything else?*	Ou bizin lotte kiksoze? *Hoo bee-zein lot kick-soze?*
Essayez-le. *Try it on.*	Seye li. *Say-ye lee.*
Je n'ai rien d'autre. *That's all I have.*	Ça même tout mo éna. *Sah memm too moh hay-nah.*
Je n'en ai plus. *I no longer have any (left).*	Mo né pli éna. *Moh nay plee hay-nah.*
Je crois en avoir. *I think there is/are.*	Mo croire mo éna. *Mo crwar moh hay-nah.*
C'est pour un cadeau? *Is it for a gift?*	Pou aine cadeau? *Poo an ka-doh?*
Je vous l'enveloppe? *Do you want me to wrap it up?*	Mo enveloppe li? *Moh hanv-lop lee?*
C'est tout? *That's all?*	Ça même tout? *Sah memm too?*
Ça vous va? *Does it suit you?*	Li correk? *Lee correk?*
Vous en voulez combien? *How much/many do you want?*	Ou bizin comié? *Hoo bees-hein koh-mee-yeah?*
Repassez demain. *Come back tomorrow.*	Répassé dimé. *Ray-pah-say dee-may.*

À LA BOUTIQUE/AT THE SHOP

Je voudrais … *I want/need …*	Mo oulé … *Moh hoo-lay …*
des boîtes de conserve *some canned food*	boîtes conserves *bwat konserv*
une boîte d'allumettes *a box of matches*	aine boîte zalimettes *an bwat zah-lee-met*
un paquet de bougies *a packet of candles*	aine paquet la bouzie *an packay lah boo-zee*
un paquet de cigarettes *a packet of cigarettes*	aine paquet cigarettes *an packay cigaret*
un paquet de tabac de pipe *a packet of pipe tobacco*	aine paquet tabac pou pipe *an packay tah-bah poo pip*
des cigares *cigars*	cigares *see-gar*
une boîte de poudre *a box of face-powder*	aine boîte la poude *an bwat lah pood*
des épingles de sûreté *safety-pins*	zépingues dé sireté *zay-peng day seer-tay*
des bâtonnets *cotton buds*	bâtonnets *bah-ton-nay*
de la crème à raser *a shaving-cream*	la crème rasé *lah cream rah-zay*
des savonnettes *some toilet soaps*	savonnettes *sah-voh-net*
un déodorant *a deodorant*	déodorant *day-o-doh-ran*
une lotion après rasage *an after-shave lotion*	lotion rasé *aftershave*
une boîte de dentifrice *a toothpaste*	aine tib dentifrice *an teeb den-tee-freece*
de la crème pour les mains *a hand-cream*	la crème pou la main. *lah crem pou lah mein*
une crème solaire *a suntan lotion*	la crème soleil *lah crem soh-layee*

French / English	Creole / Pronunciation
une boîte de kleenex *some tissues*	aine boîte kleenex *an bwat kleenex*
un démaquillant *a make-up remover*	aine la crème pou démaquillé *an lah crem poo day-mah-kee-yeah*
des lames de rasoir *some razor blades*	lame rasoir *lam rah-zwar*
des enveloppes *some envelopes*	hein pé l'enveloppe *hain-pay lanve-lop*
du papier à lettres *some writing paper*	papier écrire *pah-pee-yeah hay-kreer*
de la lessive *(some) washing powder*	la poude lave linze *lah pood lav leinze*
du liquide pour la vaisselle *a liquid detergent for washing*	savon liquide pou lave vaisselle *sav-hon lee-kid pou lahv vessel*

Avez-vous …?
Do you have/sell …?

Ou éna …?
Hoo hay-nay …?

French / English	Creole / Pronunciation
une lampe de poche *torches*	torche *torch*
des piles *batteries*	piles *pill*
une lampe à gaz *gas-lamps*	la lampe gaz *lah lamp gahz*
une corde à linge *washing-lines*	la corde pou mette linze sec *lah kord poo met leinze sek*
de la ficelle *string*	la ficelle *lah fee-sail*
des goblets/assiettes à jeter *any disposable cups/plates*	goblets/lasiette carton *gob-lay lah-see-aite kar-ton*
un fusible *a fuse*	aine fizible *an fee-zeeb*
des ampoules *light bulbs*	globes *glob*

un décapsuleur *a bottle opener*	aine décapsilataire *enn day-cap-see-lah-tair*
un tire-bouchon *a corkscrew*	aine tire-bousson *enn teer-booss-son*
des torchons *drying-up cloth*	torson *torss-son*
des oeufs *eggs*	dizeffe *dee-zef*
des jus de fruits *fruit juice*	zi frit *zee free*
de l'eau minérale *mineral water*	délo minéral *day loh mee-nay-ral*
de la confiture *jam*	confitire/lazélé *kon-fee-teer/laz-lay*
des produits surgelés *frozen foods*	produit conzélé *pro-dwit kon-zay-lay*
des yaourts *yogurts*	yaourt *yah-oor*
des bonbons *sweets*	bonbon *bonbon*
des pâtes *spaghetti*	macaroni/spaghetti *macaroni/spa-get-tee*
du vin mousseux *sparkling wine*	di vin moussé *dee vein moo-say*
du vin doux *sweet wine*	di vin doux *dee vein doo*
du champagne *champagne*	sampagne *samp-pagne*
de la bière *beer/ale*	la bière *lah bee-yee-air*
du soda *soda-water*	soda *soda*
du whisky *whisky*	whisky *whisky*

Chez le garagiste/At the garage

Quoi dire/What to say

Ma voiture est en panne. *My car has broken down.*	Mo loto en panne. *Moh loh-toh han pann.*
Pouvez-vous me dépanner? *Could you have a look at it?*	Ou capave dépanne moi? *Hoo kah-pav day-pann mwa?*
Voyez ce qui ne va pas. *See what's wrong with it.*	Guetté qui pas bon marsé. *Gait-tay kee pah correk mar-say.*
Ma voiture ne démarre pas. *My car won't start.*	Mo loto pas lé prend en marse. *Moh loh-toh pah-lay pran han marse.*
La batterie est à plat. *The battery is discharged.*	Batterie fine plate. *Bat-ree finn platt.*
Le tuyau d'échappement est cassé. *The exhaust pipe is broken.*	Tuyau d'échappement fine cassé. *Tee-ho day-sap-man feen kass-say.*
Je n'arrive pas à embrayer. *I can't let in the clutch.*	Mo pas capave embrayé. *Moh pah kah-pav ham-bray-yeah.*
Les freins sont percés. *The brakes are broken.*	Freins fine percé. *Frain finn per-say.*
Les fusibles ont sauté. *The fuse has gone.*	Fizibe fine sauté. *Fee-zeeb finn sot-tay.*
Les clignotants ne fonctionnent plus. *The indicators do not work.*	Flashaire pas pé travaille. *Flashers pah pay tra-vayee.*
Le démarreur est coincé. *The starter is jammed.*	Startaire fine bloqué. *Starter finn blockay.*

Il y a une fuite dans le radiateur.
The radiator is leaking.

Ena aine fitte dans radiatère.
Hay-nah aine fit dan rah-dee-ha-tair.

Pouvez-vous faire remorquer ma voiture?
Can you tow the car?

Ou capave faire rémorque mo loto?
Hoo kah-pav fair ray-morck moh loh-toh?

Il faut faire les vidanges.
You must do the servicing.

Bizin faire vidanze.
Bees-hein fair vee-danz.

Il faut changer les bougies.
You must change the sparkling plugs.

Bizin sanz ban la bouzie.
Bees-hein sanze bann lah boo-zee.

Le moteur grippe.
The engine is misfiring.

Motère pé raté.
Moh-tair pay rah-tay.

Il faut graisser le moteur.
The engine needs to be lubricated.

Bizin graisse motère.
Bees-hein grayss moh-tair.

Il y a du bruit dans le moteur.
There is a rattling in the engine.

Ena aine tapaze dans motère.
Hay-nah an tap-az dan moh-tair.

Le carburateur est bouché.
The carburator is choked.

Carbiratère boussé.
Car-bee-rah-tair boo-say.

Le gicleur du carburateur est bouché.
The spray nozzle of the carburator is choked.

Ziclair boussé.

Zee-clair boo-say.

Réactions probables/Likely reactions

Qu'est-ce qui ne va pas? *What's the matter with it?*	Qui fine cassé?/Qui pa marsé? *Kee finn kas-say?/Kee pa mar-say*
Je peux vous la réparer tout de suite. *I can repair it for you at once.*	Mo capave répare li dé suite. *Moh kah-pav ray-pare lee day suite.*
Les mécaniciens sont tous pris. *All the mechanics are busy.*	Tout banne mécaniciens okipé. *Too bann may-ka-nee-see-hein okipay.*
Attendez un peu. *You'll have to wait a minute.*	Ou bizin atane aine ti pé. *Hoo bee-zein at-tan an tee pay.*
Vous devez laisser la voiture. *You'll have to leave the car.*	Ou bizin laisse ou loto. *Hoo bees-hein layss hoo loh-toh.*
Garez-vous au coin. J'arrive. *Park your car in the corner. I'm coming.*	Park dan coin. Mo vini. *Park dan kwen. Moh vee-nee.*
Laissez vos clés. *Leave your keys.*	Laise ou la clé. *Layss hoo lah clay.*
La voiture sera prête dans une heure. *The car will be ready in an hour.*	Loto la pou paré dans ine air. *Loh-toh lah pa-ray dan in air.*
Ça va vous coûter ... *It will cost you ...*	Li pou coûte ou ... *Lee poo koot hoo ...*

LA STATION-SERVICE/THE FILLING-STATION

Faîtes le plein, s'il vous plaît. *Fill it up, please.*	Rempli teinke s'il vous plaît. *Ram-plee tank seel-voo-play.*
Quatre litres d'essence. *Four litres of petrol/gas.*	Catte lites l'essence. *Cat lit lay-sanss.*
Deux litres de ... *Two litres of ...*	Dé lites ... *Day lit ...*
super *premium*	sipère *see-pair*
gas-oil *diesel*	diésel *diesel*
C'est combien un litre d'essence? *How much is a litre of petrol/gas?*	Comié aine lite l'esence? *Ko-mee-yeah an lit lay-sanss?*
Vérifiez ... je vous prie *Please check ...*	Tchaik .... s'il vous plaît *Check ... seel-voo play*
les pneus *the tyres*	banne la roue *bann lah roo*
l'huile *the oil*	di luile *dee lwill*
le radiateur *the radiator*	radiatère *rah-dee-ha-tair*
Pouvez-vous ...? *Could you ...?*	Ou capave ...? *Hoo kah-pav ...?*
mettre un peu d'eau dans le radiateur *put some water in the radiator*	mette hein pé dilo dans radiatère *met hein pay dee-loh dans rah-dee-ha-tair*
mettre un peu de pression	mette hein pé pression dans ...
put some pressure in ...	*met hein pa pray-see-hon dan ...*
les pneus *the tyres*	banne la roue *bann lah roo*

French / English	Creole / Pronunciation
la roue avant droite *the front-right wheel*	la roue divan à droite *lah roo dee-van ah drwatt*
la roue arrière gauche *the left back wheel*	la roue derrière à gosse *Lah roo day-ree-yeah-air ah goss*
nettoyer le pare-brise *clean the windscreen*	nettoye pare-brise *net-toh-haye par-breeze*
Pouvez-vous m'aider ...? *Could you help me ...?*	Ou capave aide moi ...? *Hoo kah-pav aid mwa ...?*
j'ai une crevaison *I have a puncture*	mo fine gagne aine fitte *moh finn gah-ee an fitt*
les pneus ne sont pas assez gonflés *the tyres are slack*	bann lah roo pa ha-say gon-flay *bann lah roo pah ha-say-gon-flay*
Faites-vous des réparations? *Do you do repairs?*	Ou faire réparation? *Hoo fair ray-pah-rah-see-hon?*
Avez-vous un cric à me passer? *Do you have a jack to lend me?*	Ou éna aine verrin pou prête moi? *Hoo hay-nah an vay-rein poo prayt mwah?*
Pouvez-vous ...? *Could you ...?*	Ou capave ...? *Hoo kah-pav ...?*
me faire avoir un bidon vide *lend me an empty can*	faire mo gagne aine gallon vide *fair mwah gah-ee an gah-lon vid*
me passer une roue de secours *lend me a spare wheel*	prête moi aine steppe-né *praytt mwah an stepney*
m'aider à pousser la voiture *help me to push the car*	aide moi pousse sa loto la *aid mwah pooss sah loh-toh lah*
réparer mon pneu *repair my tyre*	répare mo la roue *ray-pay moh lah-roo*

Combien de temps prendra la réparation?
How long will the repair take?

Comié lé temps réparation la pou prend?
Ko-mee-yeah lay tan ray-pa-rah-see-hon lah poo pran?

Voici votre argent.
Here's your money.

Ala ou casse.
Ha-lah hoo cass.

Gardez la monnaie!
Keep the change!

Garde lé sanze/ti la monnaie/ ti kass.
Guard lay sanz/tee lah money/ tee kass.

À L'OFFICE DU TOURISME/ AT THE TOURIST-OFFICE

Je suis en vacances ici. Je voudrais certains renseignements.
I'm on holiday here. I'd like to have a few pieces of information.

Mo han vacance ici. Mo oulé hein-pé renseignements.
Moh han vah-kans he-see. Moh hoo-lay hein-pay ren-seign-man.

Avez-vous une liste ....?
Have you got a list ...?

Ou éna la lisse ...?
Hoo hay-nah an lah liss ...?

d'hôtels
of hotels

l'hôtel
loh-tell

de restaurants
of restaurants

restaurants
rayss-toh-ran

de pensions de famille
of boarding houses

pension fami
pan-see-on fah-mee

Quelles sont les facilités de logement qu'on a?
What are the accomodation facilities available?

Qui facilité lozement éna?
Kee fah-see-lee-tay loze-man hay-nah?

Disposez-vous ...?
Do you have ...?

Ou éna ...?
Hoo hay-nah ...?

d'une carte routière
a road-map

aine mappe banne la ri
an map bann lah ree

d'un plan de la ville
a town map

aine mappe la ville
an map lah vill

de guides
guide books

banne guides
bann geed

de brochures sur les ... *booklets on ...*	banne brosire lor ... *bann broh-seer lor ...*
villes principales *the main towns*	gran la ville *gran lah vill*
endroits à voir *sightseeing*	l'endroit pou visité *lan-drawh poo vee-zee-tay*
régions importantes *important areas*	l'endroit important *lan-drwah hein-por-tan*
particularités de l'île *the pecularities of the island*	l'endroit typique *lan-drwah tee-pick*
Pourriez-vous me faire avoir une liste d'hôtel ...? *Could I have a list of the hotels...?*	Ou capave faire moi gaigne aine la lisse l'hotel ...? *Hoo kah-pav fair mwa gah-ee an lah liss loh-tell ...?*
dans les centres villes *in the town-cenres*	dans sante la ville *dan sant lah vill*
au bord de la mer *at the seaside*	dans bord la mer *dan bor lah mair*
dans la région nord du pays *in the northern part of the country*	dans rézion lé nord *day ray-zee-on lay nord*
dans la région sud du pays *in the southern part of the country*	dans rézion lé side *dans ray-zee-on lay sid*
dans la capital *in the capital*	dans capitale *dan Port Louis*
Puis-je faire une réservation d'ici? *Is it posible for me to make a reservation from here?*	Mo capave faire aine réservation dépi ici? *Moh kah-pav faire an ray-zair -vah-see-on day-pee he-see?*
Pouvez-vous me recommander ...? *Could you recommend me ...?*	Ou capave récommanne moi ...? *Hoo kah-pav ray-co-mann mwa ...?*
un hôtel bon marché *a cheap hotel*	aine l'hotel bo marsé *an lah-tell boh mar-say*
un hôtel à cinq étoiles *a five-star hotel*	aine l'hotel cinq zétoiles *an loh-tell sank zay-twal*

un restaurant bon marché *a cheap restaurant*	aine restaurant bo marsé *an rayss-toh-ran boh mar-say*
un restaurant où on mange bien *a good-cooking restaurant*	aine restaurant cotte manze bien *an rayss-toh-ran cot manz bee-yen*
un restaurant végétarien *a vegetarian restaurant*	aine restaurant vézétarien *an rayss-toh-ran vay-zay-tah-ree-yen*
un restaurant chinois/indien *a Chinese/Indian restaurant*	aine restaurant sinois/indien *an rayss-toh-ran see-nwah/hein-dee-hein*

Y a-t-il des ...? *Are there ...?*	Ena ...? *Hay-nah ...?*
tours organisés *organised tours*	bane tours organisés *bann toor or-gah-nee-zay*
excursions en montagne *mountain excursions*	banne exkirsion dans montagne *bann ex-keer-see-hon dan mon-tah-gee*
parties de pêche organisées *organised fishing parties*	banne partie la pesse organisé *bann par-tee lah pess or-gah-nee-zay*
voyages organisés sur les îles avoisinantes *organized trips to the neighbouring isles*	bane voyazes organisé lor banne l'île avoisinant *bann voy-az or-gah-nee-zay lor banne lill ah-voy-zee-nan.*

Peut-on faire ...? *Can one practise ...?*	Capave faire ...? *Kah-pav fair ...?*
de la pêche sous-marine *underwater fishing*	la pesse sous-marine *lah pess soo-mah-reen*
du ski-nautique *water-skiing*	ski-nautique *ski-no-tick*
du camping *can one go camping?*	camping *camping*

Merci pour tous ces renseignements. *Thank you for all these particulars.*	Merci pou banne renseignements. *Mair-see poo bann ran-seign-man.*

À L'AGENCE DE VOYAGES/AT THE TRAVEL AGENCY

Quoi dire/What to say

A qui je dois m'adresser? *To whom must I address myself?*	Are qui sanne la mo bizin adresse moi? *Are kee sann lah moh bee-zein add-rayss mwa?*
Qui est le responsable? *Who is the one in charge?*	Qui sanne la responsable? *Kee sann lah rays-pon-sab?*
C'est pour confirmer mon billet. *It's to confirm my ticket.*	Pou confirm mo billet. *Poo con-feerm moh bee-yeah.*
Je voudrais avancer mon départ. *I'd like to advance my departure.*	Mo oulé avance mo départ. *Moh hoo-lay have-hanss moh day-par.*
Est-ce possible? *Is it possible?*	Li possible? *Lee poss-eeb?*
Puis-je renvoyer mon départ? *Can I postpone my departure?*	Mo capave renvoye mo départ? *Moh kah-pav ran-voy moh day-par?*
Est-ce que je peux retarder mon départ d'une semaine. *Can I delay my departure by one week?*	Mo capave rétarde mo départ aine sémaine. *Moh kah-pav ray-tard moh day-par an say-men?*
Je voudrais prendre un autre vol. *I'd like to take another flight.*	Mo oulé prend aine lotte avion. *Moh hoo-lay pran an lot have-ye-on.*

French / English	Creole / Pronunciation
Pourrais-je voyager sur une autre ligne? *Could I travel on another airline?*	Moh capave voyaze lor aine lotte la ligne? *Moh kap-hav voy-az lor an lot lah leegn?*
Est-ce possible d'avoir un vol passant par ...? *Is it possible to have a flight via ...?*	Eski éna aine vol qui passe par ...? *Hayss-kee hay-nah an vol kee pass par ...?*
la Réunion *Reunion*	la Rénion *lay Ray-neeon*
Nairobi *Nairobi*	Nairobi *Nairobi*
l'Inde *India*	l'Inde *Leinde*
les Seychelles *The Seychelles*	Sésselle *Say-sell*
Je voudrais voyager en première classe. *I'd like to travel first class.*	Mo oulé voyaze en première. *Moh hoo-lay voy-az en-pray-mee-yee-air.*
Il y a-t-il un supplément à payer? *Is there any excess fare to pay?*	Ena kiksoze en pliss pou payé? *Hay-nah kick-soze en pleess poo pay-yeah?*
Est-ce que le vol est annulé? *Has the flight been cancelled?*	Vol la fine annilé? *Vol lah feen ann-nee-lay?*
Laissez le billet ouvert. *Leave the ticket open.*	Laisse billet la ouvert. *Layss bee-yeah lah hoo-vair.*
Je vous laisse le numéro de téléphone où vous pouvez me contacter. *Here's the phone number on which you may contact me.*	Mo laisse ou aine niméro téléphone cote ou capave contacté moi. *Moh layss hoo an nee-may-roh tay-lay-fon kot hoo kah-pav contac-tay mwa.*

Quelle est l'heure du départ? *What's the time of departure?*	Qui lère départ? *Kee lair day-par?*
A quelle heure arrive-t-on à ...? *At what time shall we arrive ...?*	Qui lère pou arrive ...? *Kee lair poo ha-reev ...?*
Paris *in Paris*	Paris *Pah-ree*
Londres *in London*	Londes *Lond*
Genève *in Geneva*	Zénève *Zay-naiv*
Marseille *at Marseille*	Marseille *Mar-say-ee*
Perth *at Perth*	Perth *Perth*
A quelle heure faut-il être à l'aéroport? *At what time must we be at the airport?*	Qui lère bizin arrive aéroport? *Kee lair bee-zein ha-reev airport?*
Je voudais signaler ... *I'd like to point out ...*	Mo oulé signalé ... *Moh hoo-lay see-gna-lay ...*
que je suis végétarien *that I am a vegetarian*	qui mon vézétarien *kee moh vay-zay-tah-ree-yen*
que je voyage avec deux jeunes enfants *that I'm travelling with two small children*	qui mo pé voyaze avec dé zenne zenfants *kee moh pay voy-az ah-veck day zenn zen-fan*
que je voyage avec un bébé *that I'm travelling with a baby*	qui mo pé voyaze avec aine ti baba *kee moh pay voy-az ah-veck an tee bah-bah*
qu'il y aura une personne malade avec moi *that there'll be a sick person with me*	qui pou éna aine dimoune malade are moi *kee poo hay-nah an dee-moon mah-lad are mwa*

qu'il me faudra une chaise roulante
that I'll need a wheel-chair

qui mo bizin aine seize roulante
kee moh bee-zen an says roolant

que je suis non-fumeur
that I am a non-smoker

qui mo aine non-fimère
kee moh an non fee-mair

Avez-vous un vol direct sur ...?
Is there a non-stop flight to ...?

Ena aine vol direck lo ...?
Hay-nah an vol dee-reck lor ...?

Est-ce que j'aurai à passer par ...?
Shall I have to pass through ...?

Eski mo bizin passe par ...?
Hayss-kee moh bees-hein pass par ...?

Dois-je changer d'avion?
Do I have any connection to take?

Mo bizin sanze avion?
Moh bees-hein sanz ah-vee-on?

Qu'en sera-t-il de mes bagages?
What about my luggage?

Qui pou arrive mo bagaze?
Kee poo ha-reev moh bag-haz?

A quel terminal je dois me rendre?
At what terminal mustI go?

Ki terminal mo bizin allé?
Kee terminal moh bees-hein allay?

A quelle porte je dois me rendre?
At what gate mustI go?

Ki la porte mo bizin allé?
Kee lah port moh bees-hein allay?

Je voudrais avoir une place côté hublot?
I would like to have a window seat

Mo envie aine place cotte la fnete?
Moh han-vee an plass kot lah fnet

Je voudrais avoir une place côté couloir.
I would like to have an aisle seat

Mo envie aine place cotte couloir.
Moh han-vee an plass kot cool-war.

Quel est le numéro de vol?
What is the flight number?

Ki niméro vol?
Kee nee-may-roh vol?

Réactions probables/Likely reactions

Que puis-je faire pour vous?	Qui mo capave faire pou aide ou?
Can I help you?	*Kee moh kah-pav fair poo aid hoo?*
Ce que vous demandez est possible.	Sa qui ou pé démandé la li possibe.
What you're asking is possible.	*Sah kee hoo pay dee-man-day lah lee poh-sibb.*
C'est impossible de changer votre billet.	Li impossibe pou sanze ou billet.
It's impossible to change your ticket.	*Lee hein-poss-seeb poo sanz hoo bee-yeah.*
Il n'y a aucun vol ce jour-là.	Pas éna aukaine vol sa zour la.
There's no flight on that day.	*Pah hay-nah hock-hen vol sah zoor lah.*
Vous n'avez rien de plus à payer.	Ou pas éna nannien en plisse pou payé.
There's nothing more to pay.	*Hoo pay hay-nah nan-nee-yen han pliss poo pay-yeah.*
Je vous mets sur la liste d'attente.	Mo mette ou lor las liste d'attente.
I'll enter your name on the waiting list.	*Moh met hoo lor lah liss datt-tante.*
Votre départ pour le (10) est déjà confirmé.	Ou départ pou lé (10) déza confirmé.
Your departure for the (10th) is already confirmed.	*Hoo day-par pou lay (disse) day-zah con-feer-may.*
Vous pouvez toujours voyager sur une autre ligne.	Ou capave voyaze lor aine lotte la ligne.
You can always fly/travel on another airline.	*Hoo kah-pav voy-az lor an lot lah leegn.*

Il vous faudra prendre une autre connexion.
You'll have to take another connection.

Ou bizin prend aine lotte con nection.
Hoo bees-hein pran hen lot co-neck-see-hon.

Vous aurez une connexion le lendemain.
You have a connection on the next day.

Ou pou gagane aine connection lé lendimé.
Hoo poo gah-ee hen con-neck -see-on lay lan-dee-mein.

Vous aurez à passer la nuit dans un de nos hôtels.
You'll have to spend the night in one of our hotels.

Ou bizin passe la nuite dans aine nous banne l'hotel.
Hoo bees-hein pass lah nwitt dan an noo bann loh-tell.

Un de nos cars assurera le trajet de l'aéroport à l'hôtel.
One of our coaches will take you from the airport to the hotel.

Aine nou bisse pou amène ou dépi l'airport ziska l'hotel.
An noo biss poo ha-men hoo day-pee airport ziss-kah loh-tel.

Tout est compris dans le billet.
It's an all-in ticket.

Tout compris dans billet la.
Too com-pree dan bee-yeah lah.

La compagnie se charge de tout.
The airline sees to everything.

Compagnie pou faire tout.
Com-pah-gnee poo fair too.

Je note toutes vos précisions.
I'm noting down all your precisions.

Mo note tout ou banne détail.
Moh not too hoo bann day-tah-yee.

Soyez sans crainte. On s'occupera de tout.
Don't worry. Everything will be properly attended to.

Pas tracassé. Nou pou okipe tout.
Pah trah-kass-say. Noo poo okip too.

On fera suivre vos bagages.
Your luggage will be forwarded to you.

Nou pou faire suivre ou bagaz.
Noo poo fair sweev hoo bag-az.

Quoi dire/What to say

Je voudrais prendre un rendez-vous. *I'd like to make an appointment.*	Mo lé prend rendez-vous. *Moh lay pran rendez-vous.*
Vous pouvez me faire la tête tout de suite? *Could you do my hair right now?*	Ou capave okipe mo sévé dé suite? *Hoo kah-pav okip moh say-vay day swite?*
C'est pour un shampooing. *It's for a shampoo.*	Pou faire aine shampooing. *Poo fair an san-pwen.*
Je voudrais me faire couper les cheveux. *I'd like to have my hair cut.*	Mo oulé coupe mo sévé. *Moh hoo-lay koop moh say-vay.*
J'ai des cheveux ... *My hair are ...*	Mo éna sévé ... *Moh hay-nah say-vay ...*
droits *straight*	droite *drwate*
bouclés/frisés *curly/frizzy*	bouclé *boo-clay*
ondulés *wavy*	à côte *ah-kot*
lisses *sleek*	lisse *liss*
N'utilisez pas le séchoir/sèche-cheveux. *Don't use the hair-dryer.*	Pas servi sessoir. *Pah sair-vee say-swar.*
Je veux me faire ... *I want to have my hair ...*	Mo oulé ... *Moh hoo-lay ...*
boucler les cheveux *curled*	bouclé mo sévé *bouclay moh say-vay*
friser les cheveux *crisped*	frise mo sévé *freeze moh say-vay*
tresser les cheveux *plaited*	tress mo sévé *trayss moh say-vay*

Faites-moi ... *Make me ...*	Faire ... *Fair ...*
une mise en plis *a setting*	aine mise en plis *an meeze han plee*
une ondulation permanente *a permanent wave*	aine permanente *an pair-mah-nante*
un brossage *a brushing*	aine brushing *an brushing*
Vous avez de belles perruques. Elles sont à vendre? *You've got beautiful wigs. Are you selling them?*	Ou éna zoli périque. Zotte à vanne? *Hoo hay-nay zoh-lee pay-rik. Zot ah van?*
Ça va vous prendre combien de temps? *How long will it take you?*	Comié lé temps li pou prend où? *Koh-mee-yeah lay tan lee poo pran hoo?*
Un rasage s'il vous plaît. *Give me a shave please.*	Mo oulé razé s'il vous plaît. *Moh hoo-lay rah-zay, seel-voo-play.*
Rasez la moustache aussi. *Shave the moustache as well.*	Rase mo moustasse oussi. *Rahze moh mooss-tass hoo-see.*
Je laisse pousser la barbe. *I am growing a beard.*	Mo pé laisse mo la barbe poussé. *Moh pay layss moh lah barb poo-say.*
Avez-vous une crème ...? *Have you got a cream ...?*	Ou éna aine la crème ...? *Hoo hay-nah an lah cream ...?*
pour les pellicules *against dandruff*	contre tampanne *kont tam-pann*
pour revitaliser/fortifier les cheveux *to revitalize the hair*	pou fortifié sévé *poo for-tee-fee-yeah say-vay*
pour assouplir les cheveux *to soften the hair*	pou assoupli sévé *poo ha-soo-plee say-vay*
contre la chute des cheveux *against loss of hair*	pou empêche sévé tombé *po am-pays say-vay tom-bay*

pour les cheveux gras/secs *for greasy/dry hair*	pou sévé gras/secs *poo say-vay grah/sek*
pour défriser les cheveux *to uncurl/straighten the hair*	pou défrise sévé *poo day-freeze say-vay*
Qu'est-ce que vous me conseillez comme produit? *Which product do you advise me to take?*	Qui ou conseille moi comme produit? *Kee hoo kon-sayee mwa kom pro-dwee?*
Je vous dois combien? *How much do I owe you?*	Comié mo doit ou? *Koh-mee-yeah moh dwah hoo?*

Réactions probables/Likely reactions

Mettez-vous là. *Come here.*	Vine la. *Veen lah.*
Installez-vous ici. *Sit down here.*	Assize ici. *Ha-sees he-see.*
On s'occupe de vous tout de suite. *We are taking care of you immediately.*	Pou prend ou compte dé suite. *Poo pran hoo kont day suite.*
Je suis à vous dans un instant. *I'm with you in a minute.*	Mo okipe ou dé suite. *Moh okip hoo day suite.*
Vous avez de beaux cheveux. *Your hair is beautiful.*	Ou éna zoli sévé. *Hoo hay-nah zo-lee say-vay.*
Je fais le shampooing d'abord. Et je vous les coupe tout de suite après. *I'll start with the shampoo first.* *Then, immediately after,* *I'll proceed with the hair-cut.*	Mo faire aine shampooing avant. Après mo coupe ou sévé. *Moh fair an san-pwen have-han.* *Ha-pray moh koop hoo say-vay.*
Il vous faut les graisser régulièrement. *Grease/oil your hair regularly.*	Ou bizin graisse li souvent. *Hoo bees-hein grayss lee soov-han.*
Brossez-vous souvent les cheveux? *Do you brush your hair regularly?*	Ou brosse ou sévé souvent? *Hoo bross hoo-say-vay soov-han?*
Vous voulez les teindre? *You want to have your hair dyed?*	Ou lé taine ou sévé. *Hoo lay ten hoo say-vay.*
On peut vous faire les ongles aussi. *You can have your nails done too.*	Capave okipe ou zongue oussi. *Kah-pav okip hoo zong hoo-see.*
Il faut bien les ... d'abord. *First .... your hair well.*	Bizin qui ou ... zotte avant. *Bees-hein kee hoo ...* *zot have-han.*
savonner *lather/soap*	savoné *sah-von-hay*

laver *wash*	lavé *lah-vay*
essuyer *wipe*	souilllé *soo-yeah*
sécher *dry*	faire sec *fair sek*
Je vous mets la raie ...? *Do you want me to part your hair ...?*	Mo tire partaze ...? *Moh teer par-taz ...?*
à droite *on the right side*	à droite *ha drwat*
à gauche *on the left side*	à gauche *ha goss*
au milieu *in the middle*	au milié *ho-mee-lee-yeah*
Je vous ... aussi? *Do you want me to ... as well?*	Mo ... ou aussi? *Moh ... hoo-see?*
farde *make-up your face*	farde *fard*
maquille *make you up*	maquille *mah-kee-ye*
Vous n'aimez pas porter la barbe? *You don't like growing a beard?*	Ou pas content garde la barbe? *Hoo pah kon-tan guard lah barb?*
Je vous les relève et je les retiens avec une épingle à cheveux. *I put up your hair and bind/fix/hold it with a hair pin.*	Mo lève zotte et mo tini zotte avec aine zépingue sévé. *Moh lev zot hay mo tee-nee zot ah-veck en zay-peng say-vay.*
Cette coiffure vous va très bien. *This hair-do suits you well.*	Sa façon peigné la alle bien are ou. *Sah fahson pay-gnay lah hal bee-yen are hoo.*

La Photographie/Photography

Je voudrais … *I'd like to have …*	Mo oulé … *Moh hoo-lay …*
un appareil-photo *a camera*	aine caméra *an camera*
charger mon appareil-photo s'il vous plaît *load my camera please*	sarze mo caméra s'il vous plaît *sarz moh camera seel-voo-play*
un rouleau de pellicules noir et blanc *a black and white film*	aine rouleau fime noir blanc *an roo-loh film nwar blan*
un rouleau de pillicules couleur *a colour film*	aine rouleau fime couleur *an roo-loh film koo-lair*
des diapositives *some slides*	diapositive *dee-ha-poh-zee-tive*
des flashes *some flash bulbs*	ampoules pou flash *ham-pool poo flash.*
Pouvez-vous …? *Could you …?*	Ou capave …? *Hoo kah-pav …?*
développer ceci *develop this*	développe sa *dave-lop sah*
tirer ceci *print this*	imprime sa *emp-rim sah*
mettre au point ceci *focus this*	mette sa au point *met sah ho pwein*
Photographier quelqu'un. *To photograph/take a photography of someone.*	Prend photo aine dimoune. *Pran photo an dee-moon.*
Je veux prendre un instantané de quelqu'un/quelque chose. *I want to take an instant photograph.*	Mou oulé prend aine photo instantané. *Moh hoo-lay pran an photo hinss-tan-tah-nay.*

French / English	Creole / Pronunciation
Donnez-moi … *Let me have …*	Donne-moi … *Donn mwa …*
les pellicules *the negatives*	banne fime *bann fim*
les épreuves *the prints*	banne photos négatif *bann photo négatif*
Réglez bien l'objectif *Focus the lens well.*	Réglez bien lobzectif. *Ray-glah bee-hein lob-zec-teef.*
Voici le viseur. *Here is the view-finder.*	Ou guette la dans. *Hoo gait lah dan.*
Faites-moi un agrandissement de ceci s'il vous plaît. *Please enlarge this for me.*	Grandis sa pou moi s'il vous plaît. *Gran-dee sah poo mwa seel-voo-play.*
C'est flou. *It's hazy.*	Li flou. *Lee floo.*
Vous pouvez m'aider …? *Could you help me …?*	Ou capave aide moi …? *Hoo kah-pav aid mwa …?*
Mon appareil ne fonctionne plus. *My camera is broken.*	Mo l'appareil fine cassé. *Moh lap-pah-ray-yee finn kass-say.*
Mettez le rouleau de pellicules dans l'appareil. *Insert the film into the camera.*	Mette rouleau fime dans l'appareil. *Met roo-loh fim dan lap-pah-ray-yee.*
L'ampoule est brûlée. *The bulb is burnt out.*	Globe flash fine brilé. *Glob flash finn bree-lay.*
Enlevez le rouleau de pellicules. *Remove the film from the camera.*	Tire rouleau fime dan l'appareil. *Teer roo-loh fim dan lap-pah-ray-yee.*
Le film est coincé. *The film is stuck.*	Fime fine bloqué. *Fim finn blockay.*

Chez le pharmacien/At the chemist's

Je voudrais ... *I want/I'd like to have ...*	Mo oulé ... *Moh hoo-lay ...*
un sirop contre la toux *a cough mixture*	aine sirop conte toussé *an see-roh kont too-say*
un produit pour le mal *an ear-drop*	aine produit pou malade zoreille *an pro-dwee poo mah-lad zoh-rayee*
une crème pour les coups de soleil *a cream for sunburn*	aine la crème conte coute soleil *an lah crem kont koot soh-layee*
des gouttes pour les yeux *an eye-drop*	goutes pou lizié *goot poo lee-zee-yeah*
un inhalateur *an inhaler*	aine inhalataire *an in-hal-lah-tair*
du sparadrap et du coton *adhesive plaster and cotton wool*	lastoplace ek coton *las-toh-plass ek coton*
un soporifique *a tanquilizer*	aine tranquilisant *an tran-kee-lee-zan*
un produit pour la fatigue musculaire *a muscle relaxant*	aine medecine conte fatigue misskilère *an medecine kont fateeg miss-kee-lair*
une bande *some bandage*	aine bandaze *an ban-daz*
un calmant *a pain-killer*	aine calmant *an kalm-an*
de l'aspirine *some aspirin*	aspirin *aspirin*
une crème antiseptique *an antiseptic cream*	aine la crème antiseptique *an lah cremm han-tee-sep-tick*

des pastilles pour la gorge *some throat pastilles*	pasti pou la gorze *pas-tee poo lah gorz*
de la gaze *some gauze dressing*	gaz *gaz*
une lotion anti-moustiques *some mosquito repellant*	aine lotion conte moustique *an lotion kont moos-tick*
un produit contre les piqûres d'insectes *something against insect bites*	aine produit conte pikire insecte *an pro-dwee kont pee-keer hein-seck*
un sirop pour la grippe *a mixture against flu*	aine sirop toussé *an see-roh too-say*
une seringue *a syringe*	aine séringue *an say-rang*

Qu'avez-vous contre ...?
What do you have against ...?

Qui ou éna conte ...?
Kee hoo hay-nah kont ...?

la fièvre *fever*	la fièvre *lah fee-haive*
le vomissement *vomiting*	vomissement *voh-miss-man*
des crampes *cramps*	crampes *cramp*
des coliques *cholic*	colique *cholic*
des maux d'estomac *stomach-ache*	doulère l'estomac *doo-lair layss-toh-mah*
des maux de tête *headache*	malade la tête *mah-lad lah tait*
la diarrhée *diarhoea*	diarrhée *dee-ha-ray*
des enflures *swelling*	enflire *han-fleer*
la constipation *costipation*	constipation *cons-tee-pah-see-on*
une infection de gorge *throat infection*	infection la gorze *hein-feck-see-on lah gorz*

French / English	Creole / Pronunciation
les nausées *nausea/sicknes*	nausée *no-zay*
une infection de gencives *gum infection*	infection zensive *hein-feck-see-on zan-seev*
le mal de mer/de l'air *sea-sickness/air sickness*	mal dé mer/de l'air *mal day mair/de l'air*
l'insomnie *insomnia*	insomnie *hein-som-nee*
le vertige *vertigo/dizziness*	vertize *vair-teez*
le rhume des foins *hay-fever*	rime dé foin *reem day fwen*
Que dois-je mettre sur ...? *What must I put on ...?*	Qui bizin mette lor ...? *Kee bees-hein met lor ...?*
un furoncle *a boil*	aine coulou *an koo-loo*
une ampoule *a blister*	aine closse *an closs*
un abcès *an abscess*	aine abcès *an ab-say*
Mon gosse ..., que dois-je faire? *My child ..., what must I do?*	Mo zenfants .... qui mo bizin faire? *Moh zen-fan ... kee moh bees-hein fair?*
s'est foulé la cheville *has twisted his ankle*	fine foule so sévi *feen fool soh say-vee*
fait un peu de température *is having a temperature*	faire la fiève *fair lah fee-haive*
a une quinte de toux *has a fit of coughing*	pé continié toussé *pay con-tee-nee-yeah too-say*
est indisposé *is unwell*	pas bien *pah bee-hein*
saigne du nez *is having a nose-bleed*	saignement néné/so néné pé saigné *say-gn-man nay-nay/so nay-nay pay say-gnay*
a attrapé un rhume *has caught a cold*	fine trappe l'infienza *finn trap lin-fee-enza*

Chez le dentiste/At the dentist's

Je voudrais un rendez-vous.
I'd like to make an appointment.

Mo lé aine rendez-vous.
Moh lay an rendez-vous.

Est-ce que je peux voir le dentiste tout de suite?
May I see the dentist right now?

Mo capave trouve dentiste la dé suite?
Moh kah-pav troov dentiss lah day swite?

Est-ce que le dentiste est libre?
Is the dentist free?

Dentiste la libe?
Dentiss lah leeb?

Dois-je attendre longtemps?
Do I have to wait (for) long?

Mo bizin attane longtemps?
Moh bees-hein attan lon-tan?

J'ai mal à la mâchoire.
I have a pain in my jaw.

Mo la massoire faire mal.
Moh lah maswar fair mal.

J'ai mal aux dents.
I have a toothache.

Mo lé dents faire mal.
Moh lay dan fair mal.

Je souffre de cette dent-là.
This tooth is aching.

Mo souffer sa lé dent la.
Moo soo-fair sah lay-dan lah.

J'ai cassé mon dentier.
I have broken my denture.

Mo fine casse mo fausse dent.
Moh finn kass moh foss dan.

C'est pour ...
It's for ...

- une extraction
  an extraction
- un plombage
  a filling

Mo vini pou ...
Moh vee-nee poo ...

- tire lé dent
  teer lay-dan
- aine plombaze
  an plombaz

J'ai un abcès aux gencives.
I have an abscess in the gums.

Mo éna aine abcès lor mo zensive.
Moh hay-nah an ab-say lor moh zen-seev.

Mes gencives saignent.
My gums bleed.

Mo zensive pé saigné.
Moh zen-seev pay say-gnay.

À L'HOPITAL/AT THE HOSPITAL

Quoi dire/what to say

Aidez-moi, je vous prie. *Please, help me.*	Aide-moi s'il vous plaît. *Aid mwa seel-voo-play.*
C'est urgent. *It's urgent.*	Li irezan. *Lee heer-zan.*
Le docteur vite, s'il vous plaît. *The doctor! Hurry up, please.*	Vite, aine doctère s'il vous plaît. *Vitt, an dock-tair seel-voo-play.*
Je voudrais voir tout de suite le docteur. *I want to see the doctor at once.*	Mo oulé trouve doctère tout de suite. *Moh hoo-lay troov dock-tair day-suite.*
Mon enfant est malade. *My child is ill.*	Mo zenfant malade. *Moh zen-fan mah-lad.*
J'ai une douleur atroce ... *I have an acute pain ...*	Mo éna aine doulère atroce ... *Moh hay-nah an doo-lair at-tross ...*
à l'estomac *in my stomach*	dans mo l'estomac *dan moh layss-toh-mah*
au ventre *in my abdomen*	dans mo vante *dan moh vantt*
à la vessie *in my bladder*	dans mo la vessie *dan moh lah vayss-see*
aux reins *in my back*	dans mo lé rein *dan moh lay rein*
Je suis diabétique *I am a diabetic*	Mo aine diabétique *Moh an dee-ha-bet-tick.*
Je suis allergique à ... *I am allergic to ...*	Mo allerzique are ... *Moh ha-lair-zick are ...*

Je me sens très faible. *I feel very weak.*	Mo senti moi faibe. *Moh sant-ee mwa febb.*
Je suis déjà un traitement. *I'm already on a treatment.*	Mo déza en traitement/Mo déza suive aine traitement. *Moh day-za han trayt-mhan/ Moh day-za sweave an trayt-mhan.*
Il est asthmatique. *He suffers from asthma.*	Li aine asthmatique. *Lee an ass-ma-tik.*
J'ai une douleur à la poitrine. *I have a pain in my chest.*	Mo éna aine doulère dans chess. *Moh hay-na an doolair dan chess.*
Je prends 'X' médicaments. *I take 'X' drugs.*	Mo prend 'X' médicaments. *Moh pran 'X' may-dee-kah-man.*
J'ai des vertiges/nausées. *I feel dizzy/sick.*	Mo gagne vertize/nausée. *Moh gah-ee vair-teez/noh-zay.*
Ça me fait très mal. *It hurts a lot.*	Sa faire moi boucoup di mal. *Sah fair mwah boo-koo dee mal.*
La douleur revient de temps à autre. *The pain recurs at intervals.*	Doulère la vine dé temps en temps. *Doo-lair lah vee-nee day tan-zan-tan.*
J'ai mal ici. *It hurts here.*	Mo faire mal ici. *Moh fair mal hee-see.*
Ça ne fait pas trop mal. *It does not hurt much.*	Li pas trop faire mal boucoup *Lee pah troh fair mal boo-koo.*
Ça me fait mal depuis ce matin. *It has been painful since this morning.*	Li faire mal dépi gra matin. *Lee fair mal day-pee grah mat-hein.*
Je me sens mieux maintenant. *I feel better now.*	Mo senti moi pli bien astère-la. *Moh sant-ee mwah plee bee-yen has-tair-lah.*

Réactions probables/Likely reactions

Où avez-vous mal?
Where does it hurt?

Cotte faire mal?
Kot fair mal?

Faites voir où vous avez mal.
Show me where it hurts.

Montré cotte ou pé faire mal.
Mon-tray kot hoo pay fair mal.

Détendez-vous.
Relax.

Détanne ou.
Day-tann hoo.

Allongez-vous.
Lie down.

Allonze ou.
Al-honze hoo.

Je vais vous ausculter.
I'm going to examine you.

Mo pou consilté ou.
Moh poo kon-seel-tay hoo.

Toussez.
Cough.

Toussez.
Too-say

Tirez la langue.
Stick out your tongue.

Tire ou la langue.
Teer hoo la lang.

Depuis quand souffrez-vous?
How long have you been suffering?

Dépi quand ou pé souffert?
Day-pee kan hoo pay soo-fair?

Combien souffrez-vous?
Is it very painful?

Doulère fort?
Doo-lair for?

Ce n'est pas grave.
It's not serious.

Li pas grave.
Lee pah grav.

Avez-vous cette douleur pour la première fois ?
Do you feel this pain for the first time?

Ou gagne sa doulère pou prémier fois?
Hoo gah-ee sah doo-lair poo pray-mee-yeah fwah?

Je vais vous admettre.
I'll have you admitted.

Mo pou admette ou.
Moh poo had-met hoo.

Vous pouvez entrer chez vous.
You can get back home.

Ou capave rétourne cotte ou.
Hoo kap-hav ray-toorn kot hoo.

Ne vous inquiétez pas.
Don't be worried.

Pas bizin ou inquiété/tracassé.
Pah bees-hein hoo hein-kee-hay-tay/tra-kass-say..

Prenez ceci.
Take this.

Prend sa.
Pran sah.

Il vous faut du repos.
You need rest.

Ou bizin répos.
Hoo bees-hein ray-poh.

Gardez le lit pendant deux jours.
Stay in bed for two days.

Reste dans lili pendant dé zour.
Ress dan lee-lee pan-dan day zoor.

Vous ne pourrez pas voyager.
You won't be able to travel.

Ou pas capave voyazé.
Hoo pah kah-pav voy-yah-zay.

Ça ira mieux demain.
You'll feel better tomorrow.

Ou pou gagne aine calme dimé.
Hoo poo gah-ee an calm dee-may.

AU POSTE DE POLICE/ AT THE POLICE STATION

Quoi dire/what to say

On m'a volé ... *Someone has stolen ...*	Fine coquin ... *Finn koh-kain ...*
mon portefeuille *my wallet*	mo portefeuille *moh port-fay-hee*
mes bijoux *my jewellery*	mo bizou *moh bee-zoo*
mon collier *my necklace*	mo colier *moh koh-lee-yeah*
ma montre *my watch*	mo monte *moh monte*
mes clés *my keys*	mo banne la clé *moh ban lah clay*
tout mon argent *all my money*	tout mo casse *too moh kass*
J'ai perdu ... *I have lost ...*	Mo fine perdi ... *Moh fin pair-dee ...*
tous mes bagages *all my luggage*	tout mo bagaze *too moh bah-gah-ze*
mes chèque de voyage *my traveller's cheques*	mo chèqe voyaze *moh check voy-yah-ze*
mon permis de conduire *my driving licence*	mo permis condire *moh pair-mee kon-deer*
mon appareil-photo *my camera*	mo caméra *moh kah-may-rah*
mon sac à main *my hand-bag*	mo sac à main *moh sack-ah-men*
mon transistor *my radio*	mo transistor/radio piles *mo tran-zist-or/mo rah-dee-oh pill*
ma voiture *my car*	mo loto *moh loh-toh*

French / English	Creole / Pronunciation
mon passeport *my passport*	mo passe-port *moh passport*
mon billet d'avion *my air-ticket*	mo billet avion *moh bee-yeah ha-vyon*
mes boucles d'oreilles en or *my gold ear-rings*	mo zano lor *moh zah-no lor*
Le campement que j'occupe a été cambriolé. *The bungalow I occupy has been burglared.*	Volère fine passe dans mo campement. *Voh-lair finn pass dan moh kamp-mahn.*
Je viens porter plainte contre ... *I've come to lodge a complaint against ...*	Mo vine faire aine déclaration contre ... *Moh veen fair an day-klah-rah-see-on kont ...*
Je viens dénoncer ce type. *I've come to denounce this chap.*	Mo vine dénonce sa dimoune la. *Moh veen day-nonss sah dee-moon lah.*
J'ai été agressé en chemin. *I've been assaulted on the way.*	Zotte fine attaque moi dans simain. *Zot feen attack mwa dan see-men.*
J'ai fait un accident. *I've made an accident.*	Mo fine faire aine accident. *Moh finn fair an accidan.*
J'ai été heurté par un cycliste. *I was knocked down by a cyclist.*	Aine cycliste fine tape are moi. *An cyclist finn tap are mwa.*
On a forcé les portes de ma voiture. *The doors of my car have been forced (open).*	Zotte finne force la porte mo loto. *Zot finn force lah port moh loh-toh.*
J'ai eu une contravention. Que dois-je faire? *I've had a contravention. What must I do?*	Mo fine gagne aine contraven tion. Qui mo bizin faire? *Moh finn gagne an kon-trah-ven -see-on. Kee moh bees-hein fair?*

Réactions probables/Likely reactions

Quel est votre nom? *What's your name?*	Qui ou nom? *Kee hoo nom?*
Donnez-moi votre adresse. *Let me have your address.*	Donne moi ou l'adresse. *Donn mwa hoo ladress.*
Montrez-moi vos papiers. *Show me your papers.*	Montré moi ou papier. *Mon-tray mwa hoo pap-yeah.*
Racontez-moi tout ce qui s'est passé. *Tell me all about it.*	Dire moi tout sa qui fine passé. *Deer mwa too sah kee feen pass-say.*
Comment ça s'est produit? *How did it occur?*	Comment sa fine arrivé? *Komah sah feen ha-ree-vay?*
Avez-vous relevé le numéro (d'immatriculation) de la voiture? *Have you spotted the car number?*	Ou fine prend niméro loto? *Hoo fen prend nee-may-roh loh-toh?*
Pouvez-vous décrire l'homme? *Can you describe the man?*	Ou capave décrire dimoune la? *Hoo kah-pav day-creer dee-moon lah?*
On va procéder à l'arrestation du type. *We are going to arrest the chap.*	Nou pou arrête li. *Noo poo ha-rayt lee.*
On effectuera une perquisition. *A search will be made.*	Nou pou faire la fouille. *Noo poo fair la fooy-he.*
On fera une descente des lieux. *We'll make a raid.*	Nou pou faire aine descente. *Noo poo fair hen day-sant.*
Donnez-moi le temps de dresser le procès-verbal. *Give me time to make the report.*	Donne moi lé temps pou faire aine rapport. *Donn mwa lay tan poo fair hen rappor.*

Calmez-vous ! Vous n'êtes pas en état d'arrestation.
Cool down! You're not being arrested.

Reste tranquille ! Nou pas pé arrête ou.
Rayst tran-kill! Noo pas pay ha-rayt hoo.

Je tiens compte de ce que vous dîtes.
I take what you say into consideration.

Mo prend en konte/considération sa qui ou pé dire.
Moh pran han kont/kòn-see-day-rah-sion sah kee hoo pay deer.

Nul besoin de prendre peur.
No need to be afraid.

Pas bizin ou père.
Pah bees-hein hoo pair.

La police est à ses trousses.
The police is after him.

La police pé rode li.
Lah police pay rod lee.

Je fais suivre l'affaire.
The case is being attended.

Mo pou faire suivre zaffaire la.
Moh poo fair swee-ve zah-fair lah.

Restez en contact avec nous.
Keep in touch with us.

Garde contact are nou.
Guard contact are noo.

Les divertissements/Entertainments

French / English	Creole / Pronunciation
C'est quand ...? *When is ... due?*	Quand ...? *Kan ...?*
la saison de chasse *the shooting season*	saison la sasse *say-zon lah sass*
la saison hippique *the horse-racing season*	saison lé course *say-zon lay koorss*
Quand ...? *When ...?*	Quand ...? *Kan ...?*
arrive le cirque *will the circus arrive*	cirque pé vini *seerk pay vee-nee*
commencent les réjouissancs pour la fête nationale *will the celebrations of the national festival start*	banne fête l'indépendance commencé *bann faite lein-day-pan-danss co-man-say*
installe-t-on le manège *will the merry-go-round be set up*	pou installe manèze *poo heinss-tal mah-neiz*
A quelle heure ouvre/ferme ...? *What are the opening/closing hours of ...?*	Qui lère ouvert/fermé ...? *Kee lair hoo-vair/fair-may ...?*
le musée de Port Louis/Mahebourg *Port Louis/Mahebourg Museum*	mizé Port Louis/Maillebourg *mee-zay Port Louis/Mayeboor*
le jardin des Pamplemousses *Pamplemousses Garden*	zardin Pamplémousse *zar-dhein Pam-play-mouss*
la galerie Max Boullé *the Max Boullé Gallery*	galerie Max Boullé *gal-ree Max Boo-lay*
le Casela *the Casela*	Casela *Caz-lah*
le casino *the casino*	casino *casino*
le gymnase *the gymnasium*	zimnaze *zeem-naz*

A quelle heure commence ...?
At what time will ... start?

Qui lère ... commencé?
Ki lair ... co-man-say?

le match de foot
the football match

match football
match football

le spectacle
the show

spectak
spec-tak

le film
the film/movie

fime
fimm

le concert
the concert

concert
con-sair

Où puis-je avoir le programme des courses?
Where to obtain the horse-racing programme?

Cotte mo capave gagne programme lé course.
Kott moh kah-pav gah-ee programme lay koorss?

Comment me rendre/aller ...?
How to get to ...?

Coma faire pou alle ...?
Koh-mah fair poo hal ...?

à Chamarel
Chamarel

Samarelle
Sah-mah-rell

à Le Val
Le Val

Lé Val
Lay Val

au Morne
Le Morne

Lé Morne
Lay Morne

à l'hôtel La Pirogue
La Pirogue Hotel

L'hotel la Pirogue
Loh-tell lah Pee-rog

À Trou-aux-Biches
Trou-aux-Biches

Trou-aux Bisse
Troo-oh-Biss

à Mare-aux-Vacoas
Mare-aux-Vacoas

Mare-aux-Vacoas
Mar-ho-Vah-koh-ah

à Grand Bassin
Grand Bassin

Grand Bassin
Gran Bahss-hein

à Trou-aux-Cerfs
Trou-aux-Cerfs

Trou-aux-Cerfs
Troo-ho-Serf

à la plage la plus proche
the nearest sea-side

la plaze pli près
lah plaz plee pray

Dans quels coins de l'île avez-vous ...?	Dans qui coin éna ...?
Where in the island are to be found ...?	*Dans kee kwen hay-nah ...?*
des parcs d'enfants *kindergartens*	zardin zenfants *zar-dein zan-fan*
des maisons de jeu *gaming houses*	casino *casino*
des boîtes de nuit *night-clubs*	boîte dé nuit *bwat day nwee*
des terrains de golf *golf-course*	terrain golf *tayrein golf*
des salles de cinéma *cinemas*	cinéma *cinéma*
des piscines publiques *public swimming ools*	piscine piblik *pee-seen pee-blik*
des courts de tennis *tennis courts*	l'endroit pou zoué tennis *lan-drwah poo zoo-hay tennis*
Peut-on faire ...? *Is it possible to do ...?*	Capave faire ...? *Kah-pav fair ...?*
de la plongée sous-marine *under-water diving*	plonzé sous-marine *plon-zay soo-mah-reen*
de la planche à voile *wind-surfing*	plansse à voile *planss ha voo-hal*
de l'équitation *horse-riding*	équitation *hay-kee-tah-see-hon*
Est-ce que je peux louer un bâteau pour la journée? *Can I hire a boat for the day?*	Mo capave loué aine bateau pour la zournée? *Moh kah-pav loo-hay enn bah-toh poo lah zoor-nay?*
Est-ce qu'il me faut un permis pour pouvoir aller à la chasse? *Do I need a permit to go hunting?*	Eski mo bizin aine permis ou alle la sasse? *Hayss-kee moh bees-hein an pair-mee poo hal lah sass?*

C'est combien ...? *How much is it ...?*	Comié couté ...? *Ko-mee-yeah koot-hay ...?*
pour les enfants *for children*	pou zanfan *poo zan-fan*
pour les adultes *for adults*	pou grand dimounes *poo gran dee-moon*
pour un tour de manège *for a ride on the merry-go-round*	pou aine lé tour carroussel *poo an lay toor kah-roo-sel*
l'entrée *for the entrance fee*	l'entrée *lan-tray*
le guide *for the guide book*	pou live guide *poo leev geed*
le programme *for the programme*	programme *programme*
pour une promenade en barque *for a trip in the boat*	pou aine lé tour dans bateau *poo an lay toor dan bah-toh*
pour un tour à cheval *for a ride on horseback*	pou aine lé tour lor souval *poo an lay toor lor soo-val*
Vous avez fait bonne chasse? *Have you made a good hunt?*	Ou fine faire aine bon la sasse? *Hoo feen fair enn bon lah sass?*
Je reviens bredouille. *I come with an empty bag.*	Mo rétourné brédouille. *Moh ray-toor-nay bray-doo-yee.*
Comment avez-vous trouvé le spectacle? *How did you like the show?*	Qui manière ou fine trouve spectak la? *Kee mah-nee-yair hoo finn troov spectak lah?*
Avez-vous apprécié le film? *Did you like the film?*	Ou fine apprécié fime la? *Hoo finn ha-pray-see-yeah fim lah?*
Voulez-vous faire une partie de cartes? *Would you like to play cards?*	Ou lé zoué aine partie carte? *Hoo lay zoo-hay an par-tee cart?*

J'ai trouvé le spectacle ...
I've found the show ...

Mo fine trouve spectak la ...
Moh finn troov spectak lah ...

ravissant
enchanting

bien zoli
bee-hein zoh-lee

féérique
fairy-like

extra mazik
extra mah-zik

drôle
funny

comique
komik

Je me suis ...
I've ...

Mo fine ...
Moh finn ...

follement amusé
had a grand time

bien bien amizé
bee-hein bee-hein ha-mee-zay

payé du bon temps
had a good time

passe aine bon lé temps
pass an bon lay tan

Je suis mort de fatigue.
I'm dead tired.

Mo mort dé fatigue.
Moh mor day fah-teeg.

Le nombre/Numbers

Les Cardinaux/Cardinal Numbers

Zéro *Zero*	Zéro *Zay-roh*
Un *One*	Aine *An*
Deux *Two*	Dé *Day*
Trois *Three*	Trois *Trwah*
Quatre *Four*	Catte *Cat*
Cinq *Five*	Cinq *Sank*
Six *Six*	Sisse *Siss*
Sept *Seven*	Sept *Set*
Huit *Eight*	Huit *Hwitt*
Neuf *Nine*	Neffe *Neff*
Dix *Ten*	Disse *Diss*
Onze *Eleven*	Onze *Honz*
Douze *Twelve*	Douze *Dooz*
Treize *Thirteen*	Treize *Traize*
Quatorze *Fourteen*	Quatorze *Cat-orze*
Quinze *Fifteen*	Quinze *Keinze*
Seize *Sixteen*	Seize *Says*
Dix-sept *Seventeen*	Dix-sept *Diss-set*
Dix-huit *Eighteen*	Dix-huit *Deez-witt*
Dix-neuf *Nineteen*	Dix-neffe *Deez-neff*
Vingt *Twenty*	Vingt *Vein*

Vingt-et-un *Twenty-one*	Vingt-et-aine *Veint-tay-an*
Vingt-deux *Twenty-two*	Veine dé *Venn-day*
Vingt-trois *Twenty-three*	Veine-trois *Ven trwah*
Trente *Thirty*	Trente *Trant*
Trente-et-un *Thirty-one*	Trente-et-aine *Trant-hay-an*
Trente-quatre *Thirty-four*	Trente catte *Trant cat*
Quarante *Forty*	Quarante *Kah-rant*
Cinquante *Fifty*	Cinquante *Sank-hant*
Soixante *Sixty*	Soixante *Swah-santt*
Soixante-dix *Seventy*	Soixante disse *Swah-santt-diss*
Soixante-seize *Seventy-six*	Soixante-seize *Swah-santt-says*
Quatre-vingts *Eighty*	Quatre vingts *Cat-tray-vein*
Quatre-vingt-un *Eighty-one*	Quatre-vingt-aine *Cat-tray-vein-hein*
Quatre-vingt-dix *Ninety*	Quatre-vingt-disse *Cat-tray-vein-diss*
Cent *One hundred*	Cent *San*
Cent-un *One hundred and one*	Cent-aine *San-an*
Deux cents *Two hundred*	Dé cents *Day san*
Mille *One thousand*	Mille *Mill*
Deux mille *Two thousand*	Dé mille *Day mill*
Dix mille *Ten thousand*	Disse mille *Diss mill*
Cent mille *One hundred thousand*	Cent mille *San mill*
Un million *One million*	aine million *An meel-yee-on*

Les Ordinaux/Ordinal Numbers

Premier *First*	Prémié *Pray-mee-yeah*
Deuxième *Second*	Dézième *Days-yemm*
Troisième *Third*	Troisième *Trwah-zyemm*
Quatrième *Fourth*	Quatrième *Cat-tree-yemm*
Cinquième *Fifth*	Cinquième *Sank-yemm*
Sixième *Sixth*	Sixième *Seez-yemm*
Septième *Seventh*	Septième *Set-yemm*
Huitième *Eighth*	Huitième *Wit-yemm*
Neuvième *Ninth*	Névième *Naiv-yemm*
Dixième *Tenth*	Dixième *Deez-yemm*
Onzième *Eleventh*	Onzième *Honze-yemm*
Douzième *Twelth*	Douzième *Dooz-yemm*
Treizième *Thirteenth*	Treizième *Trays-yemm*
Quatorzième *Fourteenth*	Quatorzième *Cat-or-zyemm*

L'HEURE/TIME

Quelle heure est-il? *What time is it?*	Qui lère? *Kee lair?*
Il est ... *It's ...*	Li ... *Lee...*
une heure *one o'clock*	ine air *in air*
deux heures *two o'clock*	dé zair *day-zair*
midi *noon*	midi *mee-dee*
treize heures *one in the afternoon*	treize air *in air lah-pray mee-dee*
quatorze heures *two in the afternoon*	cat-torze air l'après-midi *cat orze-zair lah-pray mee-dee*
minuit *midnight*	minuit *mee-nwee*
six heures dix *ten past six*	six air disse *sees air diss*
sept heures et quart *a quarter past seven*	sept air et quart *set air keinz*
cinq heures moins dix *en to five*	cinq air moins disse *sank air mwen diss*
trois heures moins le quart *a quarter to three*	trois air moins quinze *trwah zair mwen keinz*
six heures du matin *six in the morning*	six air di matin *sees air dee mat-hein*
cinq heures de l'après-midi *five in the afternoon*	cinq air l'après-midi *sank air lah-pray mee-dee*
A quelle heure ...? *At what time ...?*	Qui lère ...? *Kee lair ...?*
A ... *At ...*	A ... *Ah ...*

une heure et demie *half past one*	ine air et demi *in air head-mee*
dix heures du soir *ten in the evening*	dix air di soir *deez air dee swar*
Dans dix minutes *In ten minutes*	Dans disse minites *Dan diss mee-nitt*
Dans un quart d'heure *In a quarter of an hour*	Dans quinze minites *Dan keinz mee-nitt*
Dans une demi-heure *In half an hour*	Dans démi air *Dan day-mee air*
Dans trois quarts d'heure *In three quarters of an hour*	Dans trois quarts dère *Dan trwah car dair.*
Ce matin *This morning*	Gra matin *Grah mat-hein*
Ce soir *Tonight*	A soir *Ha swar*
Cet après-midi *This afternoon*	Zordi après-midi *Zor-dee ha-pray mee-dee*

LES JOURS/DAYS

Dimanche *Sunday*	Dimanse *Dee-manss*
Lundi *Monday*	Lindi *Lein-dee*
Mardi *Tuesday*	Mardi *Mar-dee*
Mercredi *Wednesday*	Mercredi *Mair-cray-dee*
Jeudi *Thursday*	Zédi *Zay-dee*
Vendredi *Friday*	Vendrédi *Van-dray-dee*
Samedi *Saturday*	Samedi *Sam-dee*
Dimanche dernier *Last Sunday*	Dimanse dernier *Dee-manss dair-nee-yeah*
Lundi prochain *Next Monday*	Lindi prossain *Lein-dee pross-hein*
Les dimanches *On Sundays*	Dans dimanse *Dan dee-manss*
Chaque jeudi *Every Thursday*	Sac zédi *Sack zay-dee*
Tous les jours *Everyday*	Tous les zours *Too lay zoor*
Depuis hier *Since yesterday*	Dépi hier *Day-pee yee-air*
Jusqu'à demain *Until tomorrow*	Ziska dimé *Ziss-kah dee-may*
Aujourd'hui *Today*	Zordi *Zor-dee*
Hier *Yesterday*	Hier *Yee-air*

Avant-hier *The day before yesterday*	Avant hier *Ha-van yee-air*
Demain *Tomorrow*	Dimé *Dee-may*
Après-demain *The day after tomorrow*	Après dimé *Ha-pra dee-may*
Avant lundi *Before Monday*	Avant lindi *Ha-van lein-dee*
Après mardi *After Tuesday*	Après mardi *Ah-pray mar-dee*
Il ya a trois jours ... *Three days ago ...*	Ena trois zours dè sa ... *Hay-na trwah zoor day sah ...*

Les mois/Months

Janvier *January*	Zanvié *Zanv-yeah*
Février *February*	Février *Fay-vree-yeah*
Mars *March*	Mars *Marss*
Avril *April*	Avril *Ha-vreel*
Mai *May*	Mai *May*
Juin *June*	Zein *Zein*
Juillet *July*	Zi-yette *Zee-yett*
Août *August*	Août *Oot*
Septembre *September*	Septamme *Sep-tam*
Octobre *October*	Octobe *Ock-tob*
Novembre *November*	Novamme *No-vam*
Décembre *December*	Déssamme *Day-sam*
En février *In February*	En février *Han fay-vree-yeah*
En ... *In ...*	En ... *Han ...*
Pendant le mois de juin *During June*	Dans mois zein *Dan mwah zein*
Avant le mois de mai *Before May*	Avant mois mai *Ah-van mwah may*

La mi-septembre *The middle of September*	Mi-septembre *Mee sep-tam*
Pas avant le mois de mai *Not until May*	Pas avant mai *Pah ah-van May*
Le mois prochain *Next month*	Lé mois prossain *Lay mwah pross-hein*
Le mois dernier *Last month*	Lé mois dernier *Lay mwah dair-nee yeah*
Cette année *This year*	Sa l'année la *Sah lann-nay lah*
L'année prochaine *Next year*	L'année prossaine *Lann-nay pross-hen*
L'année dernière *Last year*	l'année dernier *Lann-hay dair-nee-yeah*
En été *In summer*	En été *Han hay-tay*
En hiver *In winter*	En hiver *Han heev-air*
En mil neuf cent quatre vingt hui *In the year nineteen hundred and eighty eight*	En mil neuf cent quatre vingt huit *Han mil neff san cat-tray-vein hwitt*

VOS IMPRESSIONS/YOUR IMPRESSIONS

C'est formidable.
It's wonderful

Formidabbe
For-mee-dabb

C'est ridicule.
Nonsense

Ridikile
Ree-dee-kill

Trop cher.
Too expensive.

Mari serre.
Mah-ree sair

Cela me fait beaucoup de plaisir.
It gives me great pleasure.

Li faire moi boucou plaisir.
Lee fair mwah bo-koo play-zeer.

Je suis très heureux.
I am very happy.

Mo mari content.
Moh mari kont-han.

Vous rigolez.
You're kidding.

Ou pé badiné.
Hoo pay bah-din-hay.

Ce n'est pas bien.
It's not fair.

Li pas corek.
Lee pah korek.

Chouette!
Great!

Extra!
Extra!

Mon Dieu!
My goodness!

Bon Dié!
Bon Dee yeah!

L'INTERNET/LE FAX
THE INTERNET/THE FAX

Je cherche une adresse e-mail.
I am looking for an e-mail address.

Mo pé rode aine l'adresse e-mail.
Moh pay rod an lah-dress e-mail.

Y-a-t-il un café internet dans la région?
Is there any internet café in the area?

Éna aine café internet dans l'endroit?
Hay-na an ka-fay internet dan lan-drwah?

J'ai oublié mon mot de passe.
I have forgotten my password.

Mo fine oublié mo mode passe.
Moh feen hoo-blee-yeah moh mod-pass.

Comment faire pour se connecter?
How do I get online?

Qui manière faire pou connecter?
Kee mah-yee-hair poo connect-tay?

L'ordinateur ne fonctionne pas.
The computer is not working.

Ordinataire là pa pé marsé.
Or-dee-na-tair lah pah pay mar-say.

Cliquez ici.
Click here.

Click la.
Click lah.

Vous vendez des diskettes?
Do you sell diskettes?

Ou vanne diskettes?
Hoo vann diskettes?

Quelle marque d'ordinateur portable avez-vous?
What brand name of laptop computer do you have?

Qui marque laptop ou éna?
Kee mark laptop hoo hay-nah?

La souris est cassée.
The mouse is broken.

Souris-là fine cassé.
Soo-ree lah finn kass-say.

Où est le scanneur?
Where is the scanner?

Kotte scanaire?
Kott scan-air?

Ayez une copie de sauvegarde. *Keep a backup disk.*	Garde aine back up. *Guard an backup.*
Je cherche un site. *I am looking for a site.*	Mo pé rode aine site. *Moh pay rod an sit.*
Le réseau est excellent. *The network is excellent.*	Réseau là li extra. *Ray-zoh lah lee extra.*
Quel est le numéro de votre fax? *What is your fax number?*	Qui ou niméro fax? *Kee hoo nee-may-roh fax?*
Faxez cette page s'il vous plaît. *Fax this page please.*	Faxez sa paze là s'il vous plaît. *Fax-hay sah paz lah seel-voo-play.*
Votre fax est illisible. *Your fax is illegible.*	Pas capave lire ou fax. *Pah kah-pav leer hoo fax.*

Voici quelques endroits à voir:

LES SITES TOURISTIQUES

Le Réduit

En 1749 le Gouverneur français David fit construire dans un magnifique jardin à Moka, une grande maison qu'il nomma Le Réduit. Comme son nom l'indique, Le Réduit était un lieu de refuge pour les familles des colons pendant la guerre entre les Anglais et les Français. Cependant, au fil des années, Le Réduit est devenu la résidence des gouverneurs de l'île. Ce château a aussi le privilège d'accueillir et d'abriter les membres de la famille Royale britannique lors de leur séjour dans l'île.

Chamarel (Terres des Couleurs)

Chamarel est connu pour ses monticules de "terres de couleurs" présentant un mélange contrasté de bleu, de vert, de rouge et de jaune, résultat, croit-on, de l'érosion.

Eurêka

C'est une ancienne demeure créole construite en 1830, au milieu d'un parc enchanteur, bordé d'un côté par la montagne Ory, et de l'autre, par la cascade de la Rivière de Moka. Une visite s'impose.

Grand-Bassin

C'est l'un des deux lacs naturels de l'île situé dans le cratère d'un volcan éteint. Grand-Bassin est un lieu de pèlerinage pour des Mauriciens de foi hindoue qui s'y rendent chaque année en février lors de la fête de Maha Shivaratree.

Trou-aux-cerfs

C'est un volcan éteint de près de 85 mètres de profondeur et de plus de 200 mètres de large qui permet d'avoir une vue panoramique de l'île.

Les Chutes de Rochester

Les Chutes se situent près de Souillac. On y trouve des formations impressionnantes de pierres basaltiques.

Plaine Champagne

À 2425 pieds de haut, Plaine Champagne se présente comme la partie la plus élevée du plateau central. Elle offre une vue splendide des Gorges de la Rivière Noire.

Le Champ de Mars

Prévu à l'origine par le Français pour servir à des manoeuvres militaires, le Champ de Mars est devenu aujourd'hui le lieu idéal de rencontre pour les turfistes. C'est là, aux pieds des collines, que se tiennent les courses de chevaux pendant toute la saison hippique.

Le Casela

Le Casela est un jardin d'oiseaux contenant 2,500 oiseaux de plus de 140 variétés, venant des cinq continents du globe. Le Pigeon Rose mauricien, un des oiseaux les plus rares au monde constitue l'attraction principale. On y trouve aussi des bassins de poissons, des singes, des tortues, des tigres et des lions. Les arbres, les ruisseaux et les petites chutes d'eau – au fait tout le décor naturel – font du Casela un cadre enchanteur.

TOURISTIC SITES

Le Réduit

In 1749 the French Governor David had a big house built in a magnificent garden at Moka. He named it Le Réduit. As the name itself suggests, Le Réduit was a place of refuge to the families of settlers during the war between the British and the French. However, in the course of years, Le Réduit became the residence of the governors of the island. This mansion has also the privilege of welcoming and housing the British Royal family during their visits in the island.

◗ Chamarel (the multicolored earths)

Chamarel is famous for its knolls of multicoloured earths, thus displaying a motley contrast of blue, green, red and yellow, which it is believed, is the result of weathering.

◗ Eurêka

Eurêka is a century-old créole house built in 1830 in the midst of an enchanting garden, skirted on one side by Mountain Ory and on the other by the cascade of Moka Rive. A visit there is a must.

◗ Grand Bassin

This is one of the two natural lakes of the island situated in the crater of an extinct volcano. Grand Bassin is a place of pilgrimage for the Mauritians of the Hindu faith who go there every year in February on the occasion of the Maha Shivaratree festival.

◗ Trou-aux-cerfs

This is an extinct volcano of about 85 metres deep and more than two hundred metres wide. It allows you a panoramic prospect of the island.

◗ The Rochester Falls

These falls are sited near Souillac. You can find in them striking formations of basaltic stones.

◗ Plaine Champagne

At a height of 2425 feet, Plaine Champagne towers up as the highest part of the central plateau. It offers a splendid view of the Black River Gorges.

◗ The Champ de Mars

Initially designed by the French for military parades, the Champ de Mars has now become an ideal trysting-place for race-goers. It is there, in the shadow of the overhanging hill, that horse-races take place throughout the horse-racing season.

La Vanille Crocodile Park

Set up in the South, not far from Rivière des Anguilles, is this crocodile-rearing farm with species imported from Madagascar. On the premises is also a small zoo of animals to be found in the Mauritian wild. The whole place will be your delight.

The Casela

Casela is a bird park with a total flock of 2,500 fowls of more than 140 varieties, originating from the five continents of the world. The Mauritian Pink Pigeon, which is one of the rarest bird of earth, is the main attraction. Other interests are fish-ponds, apes, tortoises, tigers and lions. Moreover, the trees, the brooks and the small cascades, indeed all the natural background, impart to Casela an enchanting atmosphere.

Le Val

It is natural park of about a hundred acres in the southern part of the island. A trip through this enchanting landscape will give one the opportunity to admire its waters, its ferns and wild flowers, its trees and watercress beds, let alone its giant carps and rosenbergers which will regale the palate at Le Val restaurant. Plantations of tomatoes, onions, passiflora, pine-apples, lettuces, vegetable marrows, parsley, celery, thyme and cabbage palm extend over ten acres. The melon for its part occupies as much as half the area. In this oasis of greenery can also be found some lovely varieties of orchidaceae, a whole range of anthurium and a deer-pen.

LE NORD

Grand Baie

Le village de Grand Baie vit au rythme du tourisme. Sa plage, son lagon et les activités en mer font le plaisir de tous. Faites le détour pour le shopping ou pour déguster un bon repas dans les restaurants exotiques.

Grand Baie vit aussi au rythme des discothèques et des nights clubs. Loisirs et détente garantis.

Jardin Botanique de Pamplemousses

C'est un magnifique jardin qui nous ramène au passé colonial sous administration française au 18e siècle. C'est là que le gouverneur Mahé de La Bourdonnais établit sa résidence, le Mon Plaisir, et cultive des plantes potagères. Plus tard, Pierre Poivre, intendant du roi, le transforme en jardin botanique en y cultivant des plantes rares.

Au fil du temps, le jardin des Pamplemousses, étendu sur une superficie de 57 arpents, est devenu un jardin botanique célébre, reconnu mondialement.

Le nom "Pamplemousses" vient d'un mot hollandais qui designe un fruit de la famille des oranges.

Ce jardin est aujourd'hui connu des botanistes du monde entier pour son impressionante collection de plantes indigènes et exotiques, pour ses nénuphars géants et sa grande variété de palmiers. Le talipot est d'un intérêt particulier et, d'après la légende, il ne fleurit qu'une fois tous les soixante-quinze à cent ans avant de mourir. Dans le jardin se trouve une copie d'une usine sucrière telle qu'elle a existé an 1853, copie faite en 1953 pour commémorer le centenaire de la fondation de la chambre d'Agriculture.

Le 18 septembre 1988, le Jardin des Pamplemousses fut rebaptisé Jardin Botanique Sir Seewoosagur Ramgoolam.

L'Aventure du Sucre

Une véritable aventure dans l'histoire de la fabrication de sucre à Maurice. C'est dans une ancienne usine, transformée en salle d'exposition, que vous pourrez comprendre les différentes étapes de la canne qui devient sucre. Une visite guidée vous fera découvrir cette alchimie.

Dégustez sur place les sucres spéciaux et appréciez le vieux rhum.

Détendez- vous au restaurant Le Fangourin où on vous proposera une délicieuse cuisine du pays.

Les Vergers de La Bourdonnais

Laissez-vous enivrer des parfums des fruits. Vous pourrez parcourir ce verger à pied ou à vélo. Les arbres fruitiers exhalent la senteur des îles; les fleurs exotiques et multicolores egayent la vue ; un jus de fruits à la boutique, La Corbeille, vous désaltérera.

Père Laval

Le tombeau de Père Laval, missionaire français de l'Eglise Catholique pendant le 19e siècle, se trouve à Sainte Croix, dans la banlieue de Port Louis. Le saint prêtre consacra sa vie à l'évangélisation et à l'instruction des Noirs. Le sanctuaire est devenu un lieu de pèlerinage qui attire des miliers de pèlerins de toute foi chaque année. On attribue au Père Laval la réalisation de nombreux miracles depuis sa mort. Rome procéda à la béatification du Père Laval en 1979.

NORTH

Grand Bay

The village of Grand Bay is obviously a tourist area. Its beaches, lagoon and sea activities offer memorable pleasure. Go there to appreciate the shopping and the savour of delicious food in exotic restaurants.

Grand Bay also lives to the music of discos and night clubs. Pleasure and relaxation guaranteed.

Botanical Garden of Pamplemousses

This magnificent garden brings us back to the colonial past under French administration in the 18th Century. The Governor Mahé de La Bourdonnais built there his private residence, le "Mon Plaisir" and cultivated a kitchen garden. Later, Pierre Poivre, the King's administrator, converted it into a botanical garden. Rare species of plants are brought in.

With time, the Pamplemousses Garden, which covers 57 acres, has become a world-renowed botanical garden.

The name «Pamplemousses» is derived from a Dutch word which is an orange-like fruit.

Today the Pamplemousses Garden is known to botanists all over the world for their gigantic water-lilies and their great variety of palm tress. The talipot is of special interest and, according to legend, it blossoms but once every seventy-five years to century before dying. In the garden one can find a replica of sugar factory as it existed in 1853. That one was made in 1953 to commemorate the hundredth anniversary of the foundation of the Chamber of Agriculture.

On the 18th September 1988, the Pamplemousses Garden was renamed Sir Seewoosagur Ramgoolam Botanical Garden.

The Sugar Adventure

This is a thrilling adventure into the history of the production of sugar in Mauritius. It is in an ancient factory, converted into an exhibition hall, where you will be initiated to understand the various steps leading to the production of sugar from cane. A guided visit will open the doors to that alchemy for you.

Taste on the spot the special sugars and enjoy the savour of the old rhum.

The Fangourin restaurant invites you in a relaxed atmosphere to a typical Mauritian cuisine.

The Labourdonnais orchard.

Allow yourself to be carried away by the fragrance of fruits. You may walk or cycle through that orchard. The fruit trees give off the sweet smell of holiday-making on the island, the exotic and multicolored flowers rejoice our sight. A fruit juice sipped at the shop, La Corbeille, will be thirst-quenching.

Father Laval

The shrine of Father Laval, a French missionary of the Roman Catholic Church, in the 19th century, lies at Sainte Croix in the suburbs of Port Louis. This godly priest devoted his life to the preaching of the Gospel and to the education of the blacks. The sanctuary has become a place of pilgrimage for thousands of pilgrims of all creeds every year. Since his death numerous miracles have been attributed to Father Laval. Rome proceeded to the beatification of Father Laval in 1979.

EST

Grande Riviere Sud-Est

Cet estuaire, naturellement magnifique, est un véritable appel à une excursion. Les cascades et les gorges ajoutent une indicible beauté à ce coin de nature.

Victoria 1840

Cette ancienne usine sucrière fait partie du patrimoine national. On peut y admirer le musée d'Art contemporain et l'atelier Maniglier.

Dernier élève privé du maître Henri Matisse, Maniglier, a été artiste-peintre français.

Victoria 1840 abrite la fondation Maniglier, le musée des arts pour l'imaginaire, le Café des Arts pour une bonne gastronomie, la piscine au milieu des ruines pour une excellente détente.

L'Etoile

La nature, dans ce lieu d'excursions est d'une rare beauté. C'est ce décor qui fut choisi en 1872 par un réalisateur français pour tourner le film "Paul et Virginie".

Nature sauvage. Nature protégée. Jardins tropicaux. Forêts indigènes. La montagne et la mer comme décors au loin. Des oiseaux et des cerfs qui égayent le paysage. Vous visitez toute cette étendue admirable à pied ou en 4 x 4.

Domaine de Lagrave

Evadez-vous en pleine nature au Domaine de Lagrave. Le paysage est accueillant et la nature généreuse. Une randonnée dans ce lieu, beau et sauvage, vous fera découvrir non seulement des forêts, des rivières et des cascades mais aussi le lieu d'habitation des animaux tels que les cerfs, les sangliers, les singes et les oiseaux.

Ile aux Cerfs

C'est en bateau-taxi que vous abordez l'île aux Cerfs. Des pirogues ou des hors-bord font la navette régulièrement pour vous emmener sur cette île au sable fin. Evadez-vous dans ce petit paradis entouré d'une eau turquoise et caressé par les doux alizées des filaos.

Là, vous serez certainement tenté par les sports nautiques ou par une plongée, pour découvrir les fonds marins de toute beauté.

Un restaurant pour vous régaler et des endroits d'une poétique solitude pour vous détendre.

Le Waterpark

Jouez avec de l'eau. Jouez sur l'eau. Jouez dans l'eau.

Vous vous amuserez au Waterpark sur le toboggan géant ou en faisant de la glissade.

Vous pouvez aussi vous laisser bercer dans la piscine à vagues ou sentir les bienfaits de l'eau dans un jacuzzi.

Un véritable amusement en famille.

EAST

Grand River South East

This estuary which is a natural spot of beauty, is irresistible for a trip. The Waterfalls and the gorges add an unequalled marvel to this area.

Victoria 1840

This ancient sugar industry forms part of our national heritage. There, you will take pleasure visiting the Museum of Contemporary art and the Maniglier workshop.

Maniglier, a French painter, was the last private student of the Master Henri Matisse.

Victoria 1840 houses the Maniglier Foundation. Discover the art museum for works of imagination, the Art Café for a nice cuisine, the swimming pool in the midst of vestiges.

L'Etoile (The Star)

Discover the rare magnificence of nature. A French film producer has chosen that décor to shoot "Paul & Virginie" in 1972.

Untamed nature. Cultivated areas. Tropical gardens. Indigenous forests. The mountain and the sea as far-away backdrop. Birds and deer enliven the surrounding. You may either walk or drive to enjoy the natural beauty.

Domaine Lagrave

Escape in the midst of nature at Domaine Lagrave. The scenery is welcoming and nature beautiful. A stroll in this area so marvellous and untouched, will unveil not only the beauty of forests, rivers, waterfalls but also of the abode of animals such as deer, wild boars, monkeys, birds...

Ile aux Cerfs

You will reach Ile aux Cerfs by boat. These pirogues or motor-boats shuttle regularly to bring you on the soft sand of the island. Enjoy that small paradise surrounded by turquoise water and lulled by the sweet breeze from the filao-trees.

You will be certainly tempted by sea-water sports or by a deep-sea dive to admire the beauty of the ocean bed.

Enjoy the restaurant and the poetry of the solitude which part of the island provides.

Le Waterpark

Have fun with water. Have fun on water. Have fun in water.

At the waterpark you will enjoy playing and sliding in big tobogans. You may allow yourself to be lulled by the waves of the pool or feel the well-being of water in a jacuzzi.

A family fun.

L'OUEST

Tour Martello

La Tour Martello (au nombre de cinq à travers l'île) est une construction qui date de l'époque de la colonisation britannique. Elle a été utilisée comme une petite forteresse pour assurer la défense contre tout ennemi venant de la mer.

Les murs solides de la tour et structure ronde font partie d'une stratégie de défense militaire.

La Tour Martello qui se trouve à Tamarin a été convertie en musée. Des objets de l'époque coloniale ont été retrouvés lors des fouilles et sont exposés dans ce musée.

La Baie de Tamarin

On peut régulièrement voir des dauphins dans cette baie. Même mieux. Ils vous invitent à nager avec eux.

Une véritable aventure de rêve!

WEST

Martello Tower

The Martello Tower (five in all around the island) is a construction which dates back to the days of the British colonisation. It was used as a small citadel to ensure defence against enemies coming from the sea.
Its solid walls and its round shape form have been conceived as a military defence strategy.

The Martello Tower which is situated at Tamarin has been converted into a museum. Objects which go back to the colonial days and which have been found during an archeological search, are exhibited in that museum.

Tamarin Bay

You can regularly see dolphins in this bay. Better indeed. They will invite you for a nice swim in their company.

A marvellous adventure. Almost a dream!

SUD

Mahébourg

Ce village du sud demeure un témoin de l'histoire. Mahébourg porte le nom de Mahé de la Bourdonnais, gouverneur français qui débarqua à l'Isle de France en 1735.

Le port dans cette région offre à l'époque des premières colonisations, un lieu idéal de débarquement. Puis graduellement Port-Louis est devenu le port et la capitale du pays.

Les villages des pêcheurs, le Waterfront, les ruelles sympathiques, le monument aux esclaves, ... autant de découvertes que vous ferez avec plaisir.

Le Souffleur

Les vagues, dans leur furie, ont creusé une cavité. Quand la mer s'y engouffre, elle rejaillit comme un souffle puissant et, en retombant, embrume les environs.

On entend souvent le grondement du "Souffleur".

Le Domaine du Chasseur

La nature vous présente tout son charme et son envoûtement. Un site idéal pour l'écotourisme.

Vous découvrirez aussi les joies de la chasse au cerf ou au cochon marron. Il vous sera aussi possible de passer quelques jours dans ce domaine où tout est prévu pour vous: quad-biking, pêche, restaurant, expédition...

Domaine Ylang-Ylang

Le Ylang-Ylang est une plante qui offre une huile essentielle destinée à un parfum de qualité. Vous en achéterez sur place.

De ce domaine particulier situé au pied d'une montagne, vous pourrez admirer la mer et plus au loin, des îlots.

Ile aux Aigrettes

C'est une réserve naturelle. On y trouvait, longtemps de cela, des dodos. Aujourd'hui, d'autres espèces uniques d'oiseaux y ont trouvé refuge.

Cette île a été restaurée. Des plantes et des oiseaux menacés de disparition ont été introduits dans ce sanctuaire. Vous y verrez une flore et une faune exceptionnelles.

Musée Frederik Hendrik

Avant les colonisations françaises et anglaises, les Hollandais ont occupé l'île. Les traces de cette colonisation ont été mises à jour à Grand Port. Le Musée Frederik Hendrik abrite les objets trouvés au cours de fouilles plus ou moins récentes.

Plongez au coeur de l'histoire de la première colonisation de l'île Maurice.

Le Musée d'histoire Nationale

L'histoire de l'île Maurice est riche en événements maritimes. Ce musée à Mahébourg met en évidence cet aspect de ce passé. Des cartes anciennes, des sabres de corsaires, des vaisselles provenant de vaisseaux et même des épaves du Saint-Géran y sont exposés.

Le Saint-Géran est le navire qui, selon Bernardin de Saint-Pierrre, a transporté Virginie, de France à l'Isle de France. Le navire (qui a d'ailleurs existé) fait naufrage prés de l'île Ambre.

Dans ce musée, qu'abrite une ancienne demeure du 18e siècle, vous côtoierez à la fois l'histoire navale et la légende de Paul et Virginie.

SOUTH

Mahebourg

The Southern village stands as a witness of history. Mahebourg is named after Mahé de la Bourdonnais, the French governor who arrived in the island in 1735.

The Port in this area offers, as at the time of the early colonisations, an ideal place to load off. Gradually, Port-Louis has become the harbour and the capital of the country.

Fishermen's village, the Waterfront, attractive lanes, the slave memorial... so much to discover with pleasure.

Le Souffleur

The waves, in their fury, have opened a cavity. The sea rushes into it, gushes out with the sound of a powerful breath and when falling, the water clouds over the surrounding.

The roaring of the "Souffleur" can be often heard.

The Domaine du Chasseur

There, the charm of nature is captivating. It is an ideal site for eco tourism.

You will discover the pleasure of deer or boar hunting. Spend a day or more in the Domaine du Chasseur and enjoy quad biking, fishing, speciality restaurant, trip in nature...

Domaine Ylang-Ylang

The Ylang-Ylang is a plant used to produce essential oil from which quality perfume is made. You may buy the perfume on the spot.

Domaine Ylang-Ylang is situated at the foot of a mountain and offers in the far a wonderful view of the sea and islets.

Ile aux Aigrettes

This is a natural reserve. Long ago, dodos lived there. Today other unique species of birds have found shelter there.
This island has been restored. Plants, reptiles and birds, threatened by extinction, have been introduced in that sanctuary. The flora and fauna are exceptionally attractive.

Frederik Hendrik Museum

The Dutch have colonised the island before the French and English occupation. Exhibits of this early period have been recently unearthed at Grand Port and placed in that museum.

You will have a glimpse of the history of the Dutch colonisation of Mauritius.

National History Museum

The history of Mauritius is rich in naval events. The museum in Mahebourg brings to light this aspect of the past. Ancient maps, sabres of corsairs, crockery and even the wreck of Saint-Géran are exhibited there.

The Saint-Géran is the ship which, according to Bernardin de Saint-Pierre, has transported Virginie from France to Isle of France. The ship, which has in fact existed, wrecked off Ile d'Ambre.

In that museum, found in an ancient building of the 18th century, you will be led into naval history and also into the legend of Paul and Virginie.

PORT-LOUIS

Port-Louis est la capitale de l'île. Cette ville, construite au 18e siècle à l'époque de la colonisation française, est aujourd'hui un lieu cosmopolite. Les principaux bureaux administratifs, aussi bien que les grandes activités commerciales animent la ville.
Les lieux de l'époque des colonisations et les structures modernes se côtoient dans un intéressant parcours.

La Citadelle, fort qui surplombe la capitale, remonte au 19e siècle. Construite sous le gouverneur britannique, William Nicolay, cette citadelle, connue aussi comme Fort Adélaïde, aurait autrefois une importance militaire (pour prévenir des révoltes) et civile (pour informer la population des incendies).

Le théâtre de Port-Louis, construit au 19e sous siècle l'administration britannique, est un chef d'oeuvre de l'architecte français Pierre Poujade.
Le théâtre, l'opéra et d'autres activités culturelles ont animé les planches de ce théâtre.

Le Marché Central fut le lieu de grande attraction touristique. Fruits, légumes, textile, viande, poisson... mais aussi l'artisanat, les 'rotis', 'dholl puri' et les tisanes pour presque tous les maux peuvent être achetés dans ce vieux marché (rénové après un incendie).

Le Champ de Mars est un hippodrome qui remonte au début du 19e siècle. Il compte parmi les plus anciens au monde.

Le Vagrant Depot nous ramène à l'époque de la colonisation britannique. Il fallait avoir un permis spécial pour circuler d'une région à l'autre du pays. Autrement, c'était la punition: l'enfermement dans ce 'dépôt' pour vagabondage.

L'Aapravasi Ghat est le lieu où débarquèrent les travailleurs engagés venant de l'Inde au 19e siècle, après l'abolition de l'esclavage.
Ce lieu de mémoire fait maintenant partie du patrimoine mondial.

L'Hôtel du Gouvernement est un bâtiment construit au 18e siècle sous l'administration française. Mahé de la Bourdonnais y fit son lieu de travail et lui donna tout son éclat.
D'autres structures, plus modernes furent ajoutées à cette construction coloniale.
C'est là, aujourd'hui, que se tiennent les séances de l'Assemblée Nationale.

Le Quartier Chinois est un lieu sympathique où il fait bon flâner pour apprécier les mets qu'offrent les marchands aux coins des rues ou les restaurateurs dans des lieux de grande convivialité. Des boutiques ou des pharmacies chinoises offrent toute une variété de produits traditionnels.

Le Jardin Robert Edouard Hart est un lieu de détente. Sa verdure et ses grands espaces à côté de la mer vous accueillent en toute quiétude.

Le Caudan Waterfront et le ***Port Louis Waterfront*** sont une invitation au shopping, à la bonne cuisine et à la promenade au bord de l'eau. La rade comme décor immédiat et les montagnes comme décor dans le lointain transforment ce coin de mer en un haut lieu du tourisme à Port-Louis.

PORT- LOUIS

Port-Louis is the capital of the island. This town, built in the 18th century under the French occupation, is today a cosmopolitan area. The main administrative buildings, together with major commercial activity centres, enliven this town.
Areas constructed under French and English colonisation as well as modern structures constitute an interesting discovery trip in the town.

The Citadel, a fort which overlooks the capital, goes back to the 19th century. Built under the English governor, William Nicolay, that citadel, also known as Fort Adelaïde, had in these days, a military (to warn of revolts) and civil (to warn of fire outbreaks) significance.

The ***Port-Louis theatre***, built in the 19th century under the British occupation, is an architectural masterpiece designed by the French architect Pierre Poujade.
Plays, operas and other cultural representations have given life to the stage of this theatre.

The ***Central Market*** is a well-known tourist attraction. Fruits, vegetables, textile, meat, fish... but also handicrafts, 'rotis', 'dholl purris' and infusions for almost all diseases can be bought in that old market (renovated after a fire outbreak).

The ***Champ de Mars*** is a racecourse which goes back to the 19th century. In fact it is one of the oldest in the world.

The ***Vagrant Depot*** brings us back in the days of British colonisation. At that time, the inhabitants needed a special pass to move from one area to the other. The penalty would be otherwise imprisonment for vagrancy.

Aapravasi Ghat is the place where indentured labourers had landed from India in the 19th century after the abolition of slavery.
Today this memorial spot forms part of the world heritage.

The ***Government House*** has been constructed in the 18th century under the French administration. Mahé de la Bourdonnais made of that place his office and gave splendour to it.
Other modern structures were added to that colonial building.
The National Assembly holds its sittings there.

The ***Chinese area*** is appealing for a stroll. Food at street corners or in restaurants are nice and can be enjoyed in a climate of conviviality. Chinese shops and drugstores offer a variety of traditional products.

The ***Robert Edouard Hart Garden*** is a place of relaxation. Its greenness and vast space near the sea offer a warm and peaceful welcome.

The ***Caudan Waterfront*** and the ***Port-Louis Waterfront*** call for shopping, food delight and pleasant strolls at the seaside. The harbour as the immediate surrounding and the far-away mountains make of this sea area a well-known tourist attraction in Port-Louis.